FLOWING WITH THE RIVER OF LIFE

EXERCISE BOOK

A guide to transcending the Death Consciousness

Transcendence TOOLBOOKS
Experience Beyond Words

Transcendence Toolbooks, vol 1

FLOWING *with the* RIVER *of* LIFE

Exercise BOOK

A guide to transcending the Death Consciousness

KIM MICHAELS

Copyright © 2013 Kim Michaels. All rights reserved.

No part of this book may be reproduced, translated or transmitted by any means except by written permission from the publisher. A reviewer may quote brief passages in a review.

For information and foreign rights, contact:

MORE TO LIFE PUBLISHING,

Website: www.morepublish.com

E-mail: info@morepublish.com

ISBN: 978-9949-518-05-0

Transcendence Toolbooks series ISBN: 978-9949-518-04-3

Cover and interior design: Helen Michaels

Notes and disclaimers: (1) No guarantee is made by the author or the publisher that the practices described in this book will yield successful results for anyone at any time. They are presented for informational purposes only, as the practice and proof rests with the individual. (2) The information and insights in this book are solely the opinion of the author and should not be considered as a form of therapy, advice, direction, diagnosis and/or treatment of any kind. This information is not a substitute for medical, psychological, or other professional advice, counseling, or care. All matters pertaining to your individual health should be supervised by a physician or appropriate health-care practitioner. Neither the author nor the publisher assumes any responsibility or liability whatsoever on behalf of any purchaser or reader.

Contents

How to use this book   10

PART ONE - Teachings

Awareness of the Death Consciousness   13
Awareness of the Spirits   25

PART TWO - Invocations

How to give invocations   59
Invocation for Transcending the Death Consciousness   61
Invocation for Freedom from Aggressive Spirits   84
Invocation for letting go of Spirits   106
Invocation for Exposing Spirits in my Being   125

PART THREE - Decree vigil

Introduction to the Seven-month Vigil   155
How to give decrees   156

The First Ray   159
Pure Qualities of the First Ray   160
1.01 Decree to Hercules and Amazonia   162
1.02 Decree to Archangel Michael   164
Perversions of the First Ray   166
1.03 Decree to Master MORE   167

The Second Ray   171
Pure Qualities of the Second Ray   172
2.01 Decree to Apollo and Lumina   174
2.02 Decree to Archangel Jophiel   176
Perversions of the Second Ray   178
2.03 Decree to Master Lanto   179

The Third Ray   183
Pure qualities of the Third Ray   184
3.01 Decree to Heros and Amora   186
3.02 Decree to Archangel Chamuel   188
Perversions of the Third Ray   190
3.03 Decree to Paul the Venetian   191

The Fourth Ray   195
Pure qualities of the Fourth Ray   196
4.01 Decree to Astrea and Purity   198
4.02 Decree to Archangel Gabriel   200
Perversions of the Fourth Ray   202
4.03 Decree to Serapis Bey   203

The Fifth Ray   207
Pure qualities of the Fifth Ray   208
5.01 Decree to Cyclopea and Virginia   212
5.02 Decree to Archangel Raphael   214
Perversions of the Fifth Ray   216
5.03 Decree to Hilarion   217

The Sixth Ray   221
Pure qualities of the Sixth Ray   222
6.01 Decree to Peace and Aloha   226

6.02 Decree to Archangel Uriel	228
Perversions of the Sixth Ray	230
6.03 Decree to Lady Master Nada	231
More Perversions of the Sixth Ray	234

The Seventh Ray	235
Pure qualities of the Seventh Ray	236
7.01 Decree to Elohim Arcturus and Victoria	238
7.02 Decree to Archangel Zadkiel and Holy Amethyst	240
Perversions of the Seventh Ray	242
7.03 Decree to Saint Germain	243

The Eight Ray	247
8.01 Decree to Maha Chohan	247

| *Introduction*

How to Use This Book

This book is the workbook companion to the book *Flowing with the River of Life*. It contains all of the decrees and affirmations described in that book, and they are meant to be used as described below.

PART ONE, TEACHINGS

Part One contains excerpts from Flowing with the River of Life about the death consciousness and the creation of spirits. You can use this part to quickly familiarize yourself with the topics covered in the four invocations in Part Two. You can also meditate on part of the description before giving one of the invocations.

PART TWO, INVOCATIONS

Part Two contains four invocations designed to help you become aware of and leave behind the spirits you have created. They will also help you minimize the influence of aggressive spirits from the mass consciousness or other people. In the beginning of Part Two, you will find instructions for how to give invocations.

PART THREE, DECREES

Part Three contains the decrees used for the seven-month vigil to the spiritual rays described in *Flowing with the River of Life*. In the beginning of Part Three, you will find instructions for how to give decrees. The decrees are organized according to the spiritual rays, and for each chapter you will find a short description of the ray, including the pure qualities and the perversions of that ray. You can contemplate these qualities before you give a set of decrees to a ray.

INSTRUCTIONS FOR USING THE DECREES AND INVOCATIONS

If you are new to giving decrees and affirmations, it is recommended that you start by doing the seven-month vigil in Part Three. As you gain experience with invoking spiritual light, you can then experiment with giving the invocations in Part Two.

If you are new, it is recommended that you give the decree to Archangel Michael for spiritual protection and also a decree to the seventh ray for transmutation along with the invocations. For example, you can give the decree to Archangel Michael 9 times before giving an invocation and then give the decree to Archangel Zadkiel 9 times after the invocation. You might give one of the invocations once or twice a week or more often if you have time.

If you have a daily routine of invoking protection and transmutation, you do not need to give decrees before or after the invocation. You could then do a more systematic vigil of giving one of the four invocations every day for a period of time, such as a month. After that, you could then give the invocations according to your inner guidance.

Part One

Teachings

The death consciousness is a very aggressive force, and from the moment you entered your mother's womb, you have been exposed to a more subtle aggressive form of it, which plays on your emotions and your thoughts. It is a constant projection upon your emotional body, to try to stir and agitate you into lower emotions, that are based on fear and not on love.

Awareness of the Death Consciousness

You are in a very treacherous environment, that is heavily infused by the death consciousness. And how you can deal with the death consciousness will be the topic of my next discourse, but for now I have given you plenty to contemplate. For of course, what the death consciousness wants more than anything else is to get you to react, to engage, or even to fight or seek to destroy it.

So in your mind there was an expectation. And so you see, the death consciousness has two aspects here, that you can identify, if you think about this carefully.

One is that there is a knowing behind the death consciousness that life is an ongoing process. You know deep within your being, that life is meant to be the River of Life that is constantly transcending itself.

And thus, the death consciousness cannot completely remove this inner knowing. It can cover it over. It can camouflage it. It can misdirect it. But it cannot completely silence your inner knowing that life is meant to be an ongoing process.

But now what is it that the death consciousness *can* do? It can cause you to build an expectation of what that process should be like, where it should be going as the next step, and where it should be going as the ultimate goal.

It can do so only because the death consciousness itself is a resistance to the ongoingness, to the River of Life. And when you resist the ongoingness of the River of Life, you create a distance, a space, between where you are now and where you would have been if you had followed the River of Life. And in this distance, in this space, is where there is room to build the expectation of what life should be like and where it should be going.

My beloved, one of the aspects of the death consciousness that I wish to bring to your attention at this point, is precisely this tendency to think that you have to judge, analyze and evaluate everything that is going on around you.

Do you see, that what the death consciousness wants you to do, is to be constantly evaluating yourself and your own behavior, and the way you look or don't look, and the way you dress or don't dress, and all of these things?

What the death consciousness has done is that it has set up this earthly, worldly standard, about how you should be as a human being. And you have come to think, that in order to be a good human being, you have to live up to this standard.

When you see this, you can do what we have done: accelerate yourself beyond it. This is our joy, our desire, to have you come to that point, where you see the need to accelerate yourself beyond the death consciousness, and therefore you say to us, the Chohans:

"Show me the way! I am willing to follow the path that you have followed and that you have proven. I am willing to follow the Path of the Seven Veils, the Path of the Seven Rays. Show me the way, and I will put one foot in front of the other and follow each direction I get, even if I do not see where it leads, even if it does not exactly correspond to my expectations. For I am beginning to realize, that my expectations are indeed very limited."

"My culture, my view of life, is limited and truly influenced by the death consciousness in subtle ways. I do not see all of the ways in which my consciousness is influenced by the death consciousness, but I am beginning to see that it is influenced by the death consciousness—and that I want to be free of this influence. And I know that I am only able to be free by having a frame of reference from beings that have already accelerated themselves beyond it. That is why I am willing to follow you, the Chohans. So show me the next step, and I will take that next step."

Do you not understand, that there are beings in this universe who have embodied the death consciousness to the point, where they in a sense realize at least some of the limitations of the death consciousness? And therefore, they have determined to use those limitations to enslave and control all other self-aware beings.

Do you really not begin to see, that these false hierarchy impostors, as we may call them, will use the death consciousness in all of its subtlety to keep you trapped?

When you are a spiritual person and begin to long for something beyond what the material world has to offer, they will come in and offer you a false path, that gives you the expectation, the simple expectation, that if you follow that path, then one day you will magically be transformed into a perfect being.

Let us now take another look at the death consciousness. I need you to start looking back at your life. I need you to start recognizing, how you have been affected by the death consciousness in many ways, some obvious, some not so obvious.

Yet I can assure you, that the death consciousness is not a passive force. It is an extremely aggressive force, although it is in fact capable of camouflaging itself, so that most people do not even see the attacks to which they are being exposed 24 hours a day, 7 days a week, 365 days a year for an entire lifetime.

And even throughout all of their embodiments on this planet, where everything is so influenced by the death consciousness, that it can be extremely difficult for people to see something that is not influenced by the death consciousness.

And thus, of course, the most profound and subtle effect of the death consciousness is that when people have been enveloped in it for so long, they have no longer any frame of reference, that there is something outside of the death consciousness. And they hardly ever see it, they hardly ever experience it in their daily lives.

So that they not only know intellectually that there is something outside the death consciousness, but they have experienced it. Until you have experienced that there is something outside the death consciousness, you do not actually have a frame of reference. Intellectual knowledge will not shift your consciousness; only that direct inner experience of something beyond the death consciousness.

Where they shed certain illusions of the death consciousness, until they finally come to that point, where they can go through some kind of ritual or ceremony, and then they have that experience of snapping out of their normal state of consciousness, so influenced by the death consciousness, and experiencing something more.

That I am more than the death consciousness, and that because I am not in the death consciousness, I feel no obligation to conform to it. I have no intention whatsoever of conforming to it, and I will not conform to it.

You cannot escape the death consciousness on your own, once you are enveloped in it. Your mind has become a closed system.

For the overall effect of the death consciousness is that it is a closed system, that is shut off from the life-giving power of the River of Life, from the Holy Spirit.

The death consciousness is made up of innumerable false spirits, innumerable separate spirits, and they cannot see the Holy Spirit.

You cannot remain comfortable, if you want spiritual growth. For the death consciousness can indeed make people so comfortable,

Yet the death consciousness can, of course, also make people extremely uncomfortable. And this will happen because of the second law of thermodynamics, which is actually the reinforcing spiral, where everything is reinforced, whether it is separate or out of Oneness.

And thus, the death consciousness must become more and more extreme, until it makes you more and more uncomfortable.

But many of them have not moved any closer to stepping on to the real path, because they still consider the path offered by the ascended masters an external path, where they can do outer things and study outer teachings, but they do not have to look at themselves. They do not really have to change their own state of consciousness. And so, this is still the death consciousness.

After decades of thinking that you are on the path, you can *still* be in the death consciousness.

And you will be in the death consciousness until you do what I have talked about in the previous discourses, and realize that you are looking at everything through a perception filter.

And that perception filter is influenced by the death consciousness, and the only way to grow beyond your present level of consciousness is to be willing to have that perception filter challenged by a spiritual teacher, who is not inside your mental box or inside the death consciousness.

| *Part One - Teachings*

This is what we can offer you as the Chohans of the seven rays. We can offer you a frame of reference. We can offer you, that we will systematically challenge your expectations. We will challenge your comfortability. We will challenge the death consciousness.

And when you sense the vibration of an ascended master, that is when you attain a frame of reference that is beyond words and beyond anything that can be put into a book. It is truly the priceless opportunity, the Pearl of Great Price, to come up higher, to attune your consciousness to our vibration. And therefore allow us to raise you up, so that you can rise beyond the death consciousness.

If you look back at your life, you will see that you have been exposed to the death consciousness in many ways. Consider the obvious outer, physical action.

Crime, anybody who tries to steal your property or kill you, all of these things are expressions of the death consciousness.

And then, on an even larger scale, governments that suppress their own people, governments that try to conquer other nations. Even the entire warring culture, that has been around this planet for so long.

Why should you have to grow up being afraid that nuclear missiles could be sent at the push of a button and obliterate you and your entire country? This is an expression of the death consciousness. The fear of war, the fear of some calamity, is an expression of the death consciousness.

How many of you know people who think they are superior, because they belong to this or that religion? Or even this or that spiritual movement, or even an ascended master teaching that nobody else has, and therefore they are more advanced than those who are not in that movement or teaching?

This, however, is the death consciousness. It is the lower levels of it. It is where you think that you are better than others, because of some characteristic here on earth.

And so you see, indeed, when you come into this consciousness of thinking that you are better than others, you will automatically pay a price, as you do in all elements of the death consciousness.

Because when you enter the death consciousness, you pay a price; you have to pay the piper, as they say. And the price you pay is, that there is always something for which you must compensate.

For you see the subtle reality: the Conscious You is out of the very being of the Creator. It knows that it is out of Oneness, and so in order to go into separation, it has to justify and explain. This is the price you pay. You constantly have to maintain that justification, and when you go into this consciousness of wanting to be better than others, you are obviously instantly threatened by those who are different from you, and by those who appear to be superior according to whatever measure you set up.

Nevertheless, you see my point: you are always threatened. And what must you do to avoid this threat? You must lock in to the aggressive force – that has been around this earth since the first fallen beings came here – of always seeking to project out, seeking to control others and hold them back in some way.

Yet, you may still have a very characteristic remnant of the lower aspects of the death consciousness, and that is this desire to prove other people wrong, to see ideas be proven wrong, to see other people be somehow humiliated or exposed or put down or judged.

This is a very, very aggressive force, and I would like you to look back at your life and see that beyond the direct, obvious, physical force, you have, from the moment you entered your mother's womb, been exposed to a more subtle aggressive force, which plays on your emotions and your thoughts. It is a constant projection upon your emotional body, to try to stir and agitate you into lower emotions, emotions that are based on fear and not on love.

And beyond that is a constant projection on your mental body, to get you to engage in certain thoughts, certain patterns of thoughts, that end up forming closed loops. So that your mind goes round and round and round, because you are always projecting out that the change needs to happen out there, that other people are the ones who need to change, in order for your superior goal, however you define it, to be fulfilled.

This then, is what I need you to start recognizing, so you can see that you have been exposed to this force for many many lifetimes on this planet. It has come at you relentlessly, my beloved. Throughout all of your embodiments, it has pounded on you, pounded on your chakras, pounded on your subconscious mind. Until in many cases, as has been the case with all of us who have taken embodiment on this planet, you have been pounded into submission, you have given in, you have somehow said, "Okay, I will surrender to this, to get some kind of peace for the rest of this lifetime."

So far, you may have lived your entire life without being aware of the problem I am bringing to your attention. And so, what happens when I bring to your attention that there is an element of the death consciousness?

And so, what always happens is this: there are some spiritual students who will see this but who will immediately go into denial about it. And this will block their progress.

There are others who are willing to see their own faults, but who are so willing to see them, that they now go into condemnation and feeling guilty about it. This will also block their progress.

The death consciousness attempts to create this catch-22, where it becomes impossible for us, who are the true spiritual teachers, to actually raise you up.

When we make you aware of the death consciousness, the death consciousness will use that to hold you back on the path, to put you down, or to get you to go into denial, so that you cannot actually transcend the death consciousness.

And this, of course, is not what I or the other Chohans desire to see happen. We desire you to openly and freely and consciously acknowledge the death consciousness on this planet.

But we do not desire you to go into denial or into feeling guilty, for that will block your progress. And indeed, both denial and guilt are expressions of the death consciousness.

You cannot overcome the death consciousness by using the death consciousness. This I trust should be obvious to those who are open to these teachings.

This planet is a dark planet, where the death consciousness is very strong. And there simply is no way to embody on this planet without in some ways submitting to or compromising with the death consciousness. There never has been anyone who embodied here and was not affected by it.

Do you understand, that you simply cannot take embodiment here without submitting to the death consciousness in some way, because otherwise your lifestream, the Conscious You, cannot even enter into a physical body on a planet like earth? It simply is not possible.

Just accept the fact that you have submitted to the death consciousness, that everybody has done this, but that now it is time to turn around and say: "Okay, I see this, I accept it, how do I now go beyond it? Maha Chohan, seven Chohans, show me the way. I am willing to rise beyond the death consciousness. I realize I cannot see right now how I have been influenced by the death consciousness. I want you to teach me. I want you to show me. I want to come up higher. And I am willing to look at myself and look at my expectations and my mental images and my perception filter. And I am willing to have you challenge it. I may not be able to have you challenge it all at once, but I am willing to have it challenged in bits and pieces, so that I can gradually come up higher while maintaining some sense of continuity of who I am."

Do you see, my beloved, you are looking at my release here. You are experiencing my release, whether you listen to it or whether you read it. You are experiencing it through the perception filter that you have right now. I know this. I see this. I am not in your perception filter. I do not have a perception filter based on the death consciousness. That is why I am an ascended master.

And thus, they were trying to get everyone else to come into their religion, and they were trying to portray all other religions as false. Can you see that this is simply an expression of the death consciousness, that I spoke about, of wanting you to feel superior to others? This is not the model for the Age of Aquarius.

I need you to recognize, that you have been exposed to the death consciousness. I need to you decide, that you are willing to come apart from the death consciousness. In going through this process, you will go through a phase, where you have to set yourself apart from all of the people who are in the mass consciousness. And so, you *do* need to come apart in order to come up higher. But I want you to know from the very beginning, that the ultimate goal is not that you continue to set yourself apart. But that there actually comes a point, where now you have separated yourself enough from the death consciousness, that you are no longer blinded and pulled down by it. This is when you do not stay in your cave, but you go out in society, and you take an active part and you demonstrate the consciousness of life.

For what can we do as spiritual teachers, when you have an ego that believes it knows everything and has everything under control based on this or that belief system? Well, we must pick it apart, we must take it apart in bits and pieces, for you cannot overcome it all at once.

So you must be able to see: "Ahh, here is this piece. This I can see today. This I can overcome today. I do not need to worry about the rest right now, for I know that I have made contact with a true spiritual teacher, who can see the whole and who will take me up step by step, up this spiral staircase of my personal path."

So then, my point for this discourse is this: start contemplating how you have been exposed to the death consciousness as an aggressive force, that preys on your feelings and your thoughts, creating these merry-go-rounds, or rather these downward spirals, where your thoughts and feelings, your psychic energies, keep being engaged in these patterns, that you seemingly cannot break out of. I need you to begin to identity some of these patterns that you can see, and then, as both I and the other Chohans take you up the staircase of the seven veils, the seven rays, we will help you see more and more of them.

But for now, I need you to look at one. Do you recognize in yourself the desire to be set apart from others and the desire to somehow feel superior by seeing other people proven wrong, or their beliefs proven wrong? If you are striving to walk the path of the seven rays in order to become better than others based on some dualistic value judgment, you will only make it harder for yourself. You may actually have a great drive to walk the path, as some students do. You may be willing to make many sacrifices in order to obtain that sense of superiority. But when it comes time to give up that self that you have created, then you are faced with the full force of the death consciousness. Because what do you now face? You face the very fact that in the collective consciousness is created this enormous conglomerate of these separate spirits, and they all do not want to die.

Awareness of the Spirits

The Creator itself is beyond form, as you can conceive of form from inside the world of form. Yet in order to create the world of form, the Creator does not create a form that is separate from itself. The Creator, which is Spirit, can create a form in only one way, namely by creating a spirit, a spirit that is created in two distinct elements or phases.

This matrix then becomes animated by the Creator's Spirit, and therefore becomes a spirit that has a distinct form. This spirit is now charged with the task of maintaining that form.

The Creator creates inanimate forms that are upheld by a spirit that has consciousness but does not have self-awareness.

Then, the Creator creates co-creators, who also have a form and therefore also started out as a matrix in the Creator's mind endowed by Spirit, endowed by a portion of Spirit so concentrated, so intensified, that it makes them self-aware. So we now have spirits with awareness but no self-awareness, and Spirits with self-awareness.

Thus, you see a very important distinction. An "inanimate" spirit, so to speak, cannot transcend the basic matrix according to which it was created. It cannot consciously and deliberately transcend itself, recreate itself, redefine itself. This does not mean that the spirit cannot evolve; it can indeed evolve as you conceive of evolution in nature. It can evolve within the parameters set by its original matrix, which means that it can become more of that matrix. It can gather to itself energy, even consciousness, and therefore it can grow in power, in sophistication. But it cannot change itself deliberately and consciously.

| *Part One - Teachings*

Thus, a co-creative Spirit can create form, a new form not seen before. The inanimate spirit does not have the ability to envision or imagine something beyond its own matrix. It has enough consciousness to know that it exists, that it wants to survive and that it wants to grow by gathering to itself more energy, more consciousness, and it can even expand itself within the matrix that defines it.

But, before you ascend, you are ready to express yourself in the material realm in a way that is not focused on creating specific forms or specific experiences for your Self. But instead, it is focused on raising the consciousness – raising the awareness of the whole, raising the collective consciousness – by challenging the spirits that make up that collective consciousness. And exactly how the collective consciousness is made up by spirits, will be the topic of my next discourse.

Anything that has consciousness flowing through it, becomes animated by consciousness. What you are actually doing is you are creating a spirit. We have given various teachings on this topic already.

We have talked about how a new co-creator often takes on what we have called a pre-defined role in order to have a foundation for starting its creative efforts. Yet as you continue to co-create through that role, you gradually begin to create a spirit.

This spirit, of course, does not have self-awareness as you do, but nevertheless it is a spirit. It is a being that has a certain sense of awareness, a certain survival instinct, and therefore a built-in desire to grow.

And what is it that you have created? You have created the outer self that is a spirit. The extreme importance of the concept of the Conscious You is, that it is the Conscious You that has created this outer spirit, but the Conscious You is not the spirit. The Conscious You has not become the spirit and has not been changed by this spirit. The Conscious You is still what it always was created to be, an open door and nothing more—and nothing less.

The test that you face at this point – when you have completed the initiations of the seven rays – is simply this: Will you now let that spirit that you have created die, so that you can be reborn into a higher sense of self?

The spirit that you have created, what many people call the soul, cannot ascend. It cannot ascend, my beloved. What can ascend are the positive experiences that you have had through that spirit, and that becomes part of your causal body *[See The Power of Self]*. But the spirit itself cannot ascend; it must be allowed to die in order for the Conscious You to be allowed to rise to the next level, and go beyond the 96th level, moving towards the 144th level.

What needs to happen at the 96th level is that you actually allow the spirit you have created to die, so that you can – as Jesus put it – be born again, be born of water. When you are born of water, you take on a new self, which is, of course, not completely different from the old self. Yet it is a distinctly new self, and you consciously know that it is a new self.

Therefore, you can, while hanging on the cross, realize that nobody is going to come and save you from your own creation and free you from the spirit you have created. You are the one who must give up the ghost and let that spirit die once more, whereby you can then be born again, be reborn of fire in the ritual of the fire of the Ascension Flame, that completely accelerates your being but does so by shattering the matrix of the spirit that took you to this point.

Self-aware beings started out as you do with a point-like sense of self-awareness. And then, they gradually expand that sense of self-awareness by creating a spirit. This spirit is by

Part One - Teachings

no means a dark or evil spirit; it can be a beautiful and bright spirit, that is created from the positive momentum that these lifestreams build. Yet it is still a spirit that must be allowed to die, for the Conscious You to come up higher and come closer to its ultimate oneness with its creator, with its source, the I AM Presence in your case, being that you are in the material realm.

That is when you contribute to the Holy Spirit, the One Spirit, because now by letting the old spirit die, you move one step closer to oneness. And the final contribution to the Holy Spirit is when you let that last ghost die, and then you are accelerated into the Ascension Flame. Still, every time you withdraw the Conscious You from a particular spirit, see that spirit from the outside – see that it is not the real you – and allow it to die consciously, then you contribute to the upward momentum, whereby the separate Spirit Sparks, the individualizations of the Creator, move one step closer to oneness with the Creator. And you begin to see that this is the Holy Spirit.

There is a drive inside of you to be More, and that is why you co-create. That is why you formulate an image and then imbue it with consciousness, imbue it with Spirit. This is also why any spirit that you create has that drive to become More, to expand, to grow and to intensify.

This becomes important, when you look again at the process of how free will outplays itself. Now you begin to realize, that if you start at the 48th level of consciousness and choose to go up, then you will indeed build a spirit that has a desire to expand and to grow.

Yet take note of an important point. When you are following the process of initiation under the seven Chohans, what is the essential ability that you learn? It is the ability to draw the light of the seven rays from inside yourself – or rather from your I AM Presence – through the open door of the Conscious You into the outer self, the spirit you are creating. When you create the spirit between the 48th and the 96th level, you are creating a spirit that knows it can get light, it can get the driving force for its growth, from inside itself.

As you grow toward the 96th level, this spirit you create becomes more and more powerful in using the seven rays. If you follow the instructions of the Chohans, you will actually become more and more detached from the spirit you are creating, knowing that this is just a vehicle, knowing that it is a servant that you have created, and that you – the Conscious You – is in charge.

You are not allowing this spirit to take on a self of its own and you actually – gradually – come to the point where, as you get closer to the 96th level, you become more and more aware that each time you step up one level in consciousness, you do so by letting the old spirit die and by being reborn into a new spirit that is more than the old, because it has been reborn of water.

So as you come to the 96th level, you are familiar with the process of letting the old die without holding on to it, because you know you will be reborn as More. Therefore, it is relatively easy for you to make that leap at the 96th level and completely let go of the momentum you have on the seven rays, realizing you now want something higher, which is the other rays, the secret rays. The higher rays are not meant to create material form, but are meant to create something beyond material form and thereby contribute to the raising of the collective awareness, rather than the physical manifestations that you see with the senses.

Unfortunately, it is possible that a lifestream does not become more aware of this process of letting the old die, but is so focused on expanding the spirit, magnifying that spirit, that it is creating more and more physical manifestations. It does not consciously see that it is letting the old die.

It wants to use its momentum to demonstrate some mastery of mind over matter, that it may go out and create these phenomena that can impress those who are further down on the path. Thus, a lifestream can become attached to the spirit and decide that it will not let it go, and this causes the lifestream to fall.

What you need to understand is that when you do go below the 48th level of awareness, no matter what point you go below, then the spirit that you had created up until that point now becomes a spirit that cannot see that it can get energy from inside itself.

It instantly reverts to a spirit, or is transformed into a spirit, that now knows it must take light from outside itself. Yet it still has the basic drive that is the drive of all life, the drive that in a way is consciousness itself, namely the drive to multiply, the drive to become More.

WHY SPIRITS BECOME AGGRESSIVE

You now have a spirit that has a drive to become More, but cannot become More by getting the energy of the seven rays from inside itself. So what must this spirit do? It must seek to become More by taking energy from the level where it is at in the material realm. And that means it now becomes a spirit, that by its very nature is an aggressive spirit, that must and will take light from other spirits.

That is why you now have a spirit that cannot live and let live. It has no life in itself, the life of the Spirit. So it has in a sense become what Jesus talked about, when he talked about those who are dead in a spiritual sense, as when he said: "Let the dead bury their dead."

And they must, of course, take from without through either deceit or direct force. It is why we have, as we have talked about before, the two types of fallen beings:

1. Those who seek to use obvious force to take from others.

2. Those who use deceit, so that they can get others to voluntarily give them their energy.

Now you understand the basic teaching, that the Holy Spirit is the Spirit of self-transcendence by taking energy from the spiritual realm and multiplying the talents, thereby needing to take nothing from the level where you are at, but only giving to that level.

And you also have the dead spirit, the one that is not alive. The dead spirit seeks to take from its own level, for it cannot get from within; it cannot get from the higher level, because it is no longer the open door.

So, there is the one Holy Spirit, that always moves closer and closer to oneness. And then you have the multiplicity of the separate spirits, the dead spirits, that are in fact moving further and further away from oneness the more power they gather to themselves.

Each time they take from another, they move further away from oneness with that other. For how can you forcefully or deceitfully take from another and move closer to oneness with that other? It simply is not possible. Do you begin to see this?

What happens in the ideal scenario is, that you rise from the 48th through the 49th level of consciousness. And as you rise, you create a spirit. Then you allow that spirit to be reborn into a higher spirit, and this allows you to rise to the next level of consciousness. Take note that in this ideal scenario you are not actually dealing with the concept, that you on earth today see as death. It is not truly necessary for you to let the old spirit die, in the sense you understand death on earth.

Yet in the ideal scenario, you do not have to go through the process of letting the old spirit die, in the sense that it ceases to be, that something is forced upon you, and that this is a loss or a cessation of consciousness. Instead, you realize that you can simply allow yourself to be reborn into a higher sense of self.

Therefore, one could say that what you do between the 48th and the 96th level of consciousness, is that you very smoothly allow one spirit to transcend itself into the next spirit—and the next, and the next, and the next. This is a process that does not entail any abrupt stoppages, as you associate with death today. You are simply flowing from one stage to the next, and therefore it is easy for a co-creator to get the sense, that you have continuity between the spirit at one level of consciousness and the spirit at the next level of consciousness.

This can then give you, as I spoke about previously, the sense that you are building a continuous spirit instead of going from one spirit to the next. Yet at the same time, if you have contact with a spiritual teacher, then the teacher will prepare you for the fact, that when you come to the 96th level, you do have to go through an abrupt change. Because at that point you actually have to "lay down your life for a friend," as Jesus expressed it.

You have to have that greater love of being willing to lay down the spirit, that you have created at the first 48 levels of consciousness. For this spirit cannot take you beyond the 96th level, as it is a spirit that was focused on raising itself as an individual spirit. In order to transcend and go beyond the 96th level, you need to start creating a new spirit, that is aimed at raising up more than your individual self, that is aimed at raising up the whole.

In the ideal scenario, this is a more abrupt change than you have experienced before, but it is still not what you see as death today. Because truly, it is not a loss for the Conscious You. As you have become more and more conscious, as you grew towards the 96th level, you have also become conscious of the fact, that you will not die if your spirit dies, because you are more than the spirit. The spirit is not you. You have not created a "self;" you have not even recreated yourself as the spirit.

You are conscious of the fact that the spirit is just a vehicle, that you are using to express yourself in the material world. Therefore, you will know that even if this spirit dies, you will not die. There will not even be a cessation of consciousness. There will not be an abrupt change or loss. This means that you can, when you are aware of this, smoothly let go of the old. You can lay down your life for a greater cause than raising up an individual self. You can therefore smoothly transition into that next phase.

Truly, in the ideal scenario, you would not be confronted with what I, in the last discourse, talked about as the aggressive spirits.

In the ideal scenario, you are creating a spirit, and a number of spirits, as you grow from the 48th to the 96th level. But these are spirits that have two interesting characteristics. One is that they know that you can draw enough energy from inside yourself to drive your creative efforts. Thus, you do not need to take anything from outside yourself, from other lifestreams, meaning there is nothing aggressive in this kind of spirit. Furthermore, the spirit you are creating has the overall goal of growing towards a higher state of consciousness. You are not creating a static spirit; you are creating a spirit that wants to grow, that wants to transition into a higher phase.

So you need to find a way to either forcefully or deceitfully get other lifestreams to give their energy. This means you now create a new type of spirit, that is not focused on getting energy from within and upon growing to another stage that is higher than its own stage.

| *Part One - Teachings*

Instead, you create a spirit that is focused on taking energy from the world around it, and it is focused on expanding itself as a powerful being in this world. In other words, instead of seeking to become more than you are; you now have a spirit who seeks to become more of what it already is—more powerful in terms of doing the things you can do in the material realm.

What you now see is that since the original fall, the beings that fell into the consciousness of separation have created innumerable spirits, that are based on the illusion of separation. These are separate spirits, that seek to aggressively influence other lifestreams. Their entire modus operandi, their entire design, is aimed at aggressively taking energy from others. Some of them seek to do this through obvious force, others seek to do this through fear, and others seek to do it through deception. Yet they are all aimed at this one goal: aggressively projecting their own matrix, the thought-matrix that created them, upon other lifestreams for the purpose of controlling them.

OVERCOMING FALSE SPIRITS

You now see, that in the ideal scenario you have 48 levels, as you go through the path of the seven rays. For each of them there is a certain spirit. In order to go from one level to the next, you have to leave that spirit behind and embrace the next spirit. Yet none of those spirits are aggressively seeking to control your mind, and thus it is not a hard process—in the ideal scenario.

But what you have on planet earth today is not the ideal scenario. It is a scenario, where you now have false spirits, that have been created at each of the 48 levels of consciousness between the 48th and the 96th level.

In other words, for each step that you take on the path of the seven rays, there is a false spirit. And this false spirit will aggressively seek to prevent you from taking the next step on the

— 34 —

path. It will seek to keep you on the level where you are at, and to keep you there indefinitely.

You also have the scenario that many beings have gone below the 48th level of consciousness, which is something you do not have to deal with in the ideal scenario. Yet what you have today on earth is that many beings have gone below the 48th level, and they have, of course, also created false spirits, or aggressive-spirits, for each of the levels between the 48th level and the 1st level, the lowest level of consciousness.

What you now have is an interesting interaction between the false spirits above the 48th level and the aggressive-spirits below. You now see that in order to pass from one level of consciousness to the next, you do not simply have to deal with the spirit that you yourself have created at your current level of consciousness. You also have to deal with the false spirit at that level, and then the aggressive spirit at the corresponding level beneath the 48th level of consciousness.

For example, if you are currently 10 levels above the 48th level of consciousness, then there is what we might call a true spirit at that level, which you use as a vehicle to get to the next level. But there is also a false spirit, that justifies why you should not move from that level to the next level. And then, there is a corresponding aggressive spirit, that is 10 levels below the 48th level, which is also aggressively seeking to draw you into its matrix.

FALSE AND AGGRESSIVE SPIRITS

Here is the difference. The false-spirit that is 10 levels above the 48th level is aimed at justifying why you do not go higher than that level of consciousness. But the aggressive spirit is aimed at drawing you into the dualistic struggle between you and some kind of opponent.

The false spirits that exist between the 48th and the 96th level are still focused on you as an individual lifestream, because you are in the process of growing as an individual lifestream. So the false spirit will say to you: "You do not need to grow beyond this level, and here is why and here are all the justifications for why you should not grow. You should stay here and enjoy this level and expand your awareness at this level only." This is still not aimed at anything outside yourself; it is aimed at you.

Yet the corresponding aggressive spirit, that is below the 48th level of consciousness, is trapped in the dualistic mindset. It sees itself as being opposed by an external enemy, and therefore it sees itself as being in a constant battle with this external enemy. The lower you go between the 48th level and the lowest level of consciousness, the more you find spirits who are completely trapped in what we have called the epic mindset. This is where you see the battle between the ultimate forces of good and evil, such as the traditional theistic view of God, and the equally theistic view of the devil as being in opposition to God. So you see the difference.

There is still a false spirit, that is focused on you as an individual lifestream, but then there is the aggressive spirit, where you are not even focused on yourself anymore; you are focused on dealing with some external opponent. At some level this will be other people, at other levels it will be a greater dark force, but at the very lowest level your external opponent is actually God. Because you now think – as the fallen ones fell into the original illusion – that God has made a mistake and created a faulty design for the universe. And it is your task to correct God's mistake and set things right, by forcing others to follow you in your vision of salvation.

THE GROWTH OF THE WHOLE

You now see that, in a sense, there is a mirror image between the levels of consciousness from the 96th to the 144th level, and the levels below the 48th level. As you rise from the 96th to the 144th level, you must overcome and deal with these aggressive spirits. And you must not only overcome them in your own mind, but you must also make a contribution to slaying these spirits—to having them bound, judged and ultimately having the matrix shattered as you rise in consciousness.

Therefore, your personal growth from one level to the next, makes it easier for other lifestreams to grow beyond that particular aggressive spirit and the illusions behind it. This then is what facilitates the growth of the entire sphere of planet earth, where you can eventually get to a point, as we have explained, where the level of the 144 potential states of consciousness is raised, so that what is the lowest level right now, will no longer be allowed on earth. And the beings who are at that level, will have to go somewhere else, whereby the earth is set free from the downward pull of these lifestreams. Yet, let us not get too far ahead of ourselves, for the focus on this series of discourses is to help you grow from the 48th to the 96th level.

Namely, that at your current level of consciousness, whatever that is, you have created a spirit. That spirit is not you, because you are still the Conscious You, which is pure awareness. You have not become this spirit. You are only seeing – you are perceiving – life through the perception filter of that spirit.

Thus, it is not you who can't stand the situation; it is the spirit who can't stand the situation. For it has put itself into a blind alley – a catch-22 – where it seemingly cannot get out of it in any way that it can see. And it is perfectly true, that if you look at your situation through the perception filter of that spirit, you cannot get out of it—there is no way out. But there is a way out, and that is to realize: "I am not that spirit, I am More than that spirit." And that means I have the potential to rise to the next level of consciousness, but how can I do this?

You can do this in only one way: by letting your current spirit die! Believe me, because that spirit is an aggressive spirit, it will experience it as a death, as you currently see death on planet earth—where everything, every thought system, every philosophy, every religion – even most spiritual teachings – is influenced by the consciousness of death, the consciousness of separation and duality.

This is why you have to acknowledge a simple fact. In today's less than ideal scenario – whether you are below the 48th level or between the 48th and the 96th level – the only way to grow to the next level of your path, is that you must deal with the negative, aggressive spirit that corresponds to your current level. In order to free yourself from the downward pull of that spirit, you must look at the spirit of your self, and see it as a spirit that is different from the Conscious You, different from the real you. And you must consciously and deliberately say to that spirit: "I am not you, and I do not want to see life through the filter that you are. I acknowledge that you are unreal, and I am willing to let you die, so that I can be free to rise to a higher level."

FROM SEPARATENESS TO ONENESS

The death consciousness is made up of innumerable false spirits, innumerable separate spirits, and they cannot see the Holy Spirit. If they were to see and acknowledge the Holy Spirit, they would instantly cease to exist as separate spirits. Do you see this, my beloved? Do you begin to at least glimpse this? You cannot be separate and in oneness at the same time. You cannot have your cake and eat it too.

WHEN SPIRITS REACT TO OTHER SPIRITS

Now, when you take what I have said earlier, you should be able to see a simple fact. What is it that the fallen beings do to attack you with this aggressive force? What is that force? It is what I have talked about earlier: a spirit. The fallen beings have created a spirit that goes out and attacks you. But what do you create, when you react to this attack—whether you seek to escape it or whether you seek to fight back? Well, you also create a spirit. You create your own personal spirit. And for each step you go down below the 48th level, you are creating a new spirit.

What is it that happens, when a person reaches what they call rock bottom and says, "No, I can no longer do this?" This is when you decide that you will no longer create another spirit, and that you will attempt to stop feeding the spirits that you have created. You may not be consciously aware of this, but this is actually what happens.

So what is it that is required, for you to climb back up the spiral staircase towards the 96th level of consciousness? It is that you must go through the journey of confronting the spirits you have created and slaying them, as Saint George slew the dragon.

For you see, which part of you is it that can feel it is being opposed by the dark spirits created by the fallen beings? Well, it is only the spirits that you have created. For only a separate spirit can feel opposed by other separate spirits. The One Spirit, the undivided Spirit, the indivisible Spirit, the Holy Spirit, does not feel opposed by separate spirits, because it knows it is beyond them, beyond their reach. Because as soon as it feels their attack, what does it do? It does not go into denial. It does not go into fighting. It simply transcends itself, so that it becomes transparent to the force that is directed towards it.

So what I am attempting to explain here is this: before you can rise beyond the 48th level, you must slay the spirits you have created beneath that level. But beyond the individual spirits, there is one spirit you need to slay, and that is the spirit of feeling what I have described earlier as being threatened, as having a need to project into the minds of other people, because you seek to change them instead of changing yourself.

JUSTIFYING YOUR LOWER SPIRITS

So what is it that happens below the 48th level? It is that you go into a perversion of the upper levels of consciousness, the levels beyond the 96th level, where you now start directing an aggressive spirit. You start creating aggressive spirits, that are aimed at controlling the minds of other people. But not only do you do this, you justify this by some greater cause—that you are doing this to help God's cause and not out of selfish reasons.

This is the one spirit you must slay before you can rise above the 48th level. That is why I say to you, with as much clarity as can be put into words: "If you want to make it to the 96th level of consciousness, if you want to follow the true spiritual path, if you want to qualify for initiation under the seven Chohans, you must fulfill this one requirement: stop focusing on changing other people or the world! Withdraw all attention from seeking to change anything outside yourself. Instead, focus all attention on changing your own state of consciousness, slaying the spirits you have created and embodying the positive lessons of the seven rays, so that you build the individual self."

I have said that you may be above the 48th level of consciousness, and therefore you can more quickly catch up. But you still need to be humble, realistic and honest enough to start at the beginning, to start with the Chohan of the First Ray and work your way up, so that you do not skip steps and leave any spirits lingering in the subconscious, who will later come out and seek to devour you, for they will actually grow when they can stay hidden.

You see, the consequence of my teaching earlier – that even if you manage to ignore or deny the existence of dark spirits or the spirits you have created – is simply this: there will still be energy directed into your subconscious mind, and that means that whatever the spirits that are lurching there, they will grow in the hiding places that are maintained by your unwillingness to look at yourself.

Being unwilling to look at your own consciousness, to look into your subconscious mind, is the surest way to feed the spirits that are there. And they will keep growing, until you decide to abandon your willful ignorance and instead shine the light of your I AM Presence, the light of the seven rays, into the caves of the subconscious mind, flushing out those spirits into the open, so that you can see them. And then, with the expert guidance of the seven Chohans, you slay them one by one.

LOOK INSIDE YOUR SELF

You do not need to fear this, for you will not have to confront them all at once, and you will not have to confront any spirit until you are ready to slay it. Neither will you have to confront it alone. You are walking the path of the seven Chohans. This is what we offer you in this book and the coming books, and we have already set you on this path by our first book in this series.

So you see, you are not walking alone. You will not have to face your spirits all alone. You will have one of the Chohans with you. You will have a corresponding Archangel and the Elohim. Thus, you will, if you are willing, have all the guidance, and all the tools, and all the knowledge needed to see through those spirits and slay them one by one.

Yet you cannot even begin this path until you at least acknowledge the one spirit that causes you to direct your attention outside yourself. This is the one requirement. For you see, my beloved, a simple reality here. We of the seven Chohans, and the

| *Part One - Teachings*

eighth of myself, we are the true spiritual teachers of humankind. We have been given a task by cosmic hierarchies, and this task is to raise up the lifestreams of earth.

But what are we seeking to raise up? We are seeking to raise up what Jesus referred to, when he told Nicodemus that no man can ascend back to heaven except he that descended from heaven. And what descended from heaven was the Conscious You, that state of pure awareness. What you have created since then is a separate self, a separate sense of identity, that is made up of many individual spirits.

We, of the Chohans, are not charged with raising those spirits. This is not our job, and we will not compromise our calling. We will not help you to raise up the separate self. So unless you come to the point, where you realize that the true goal of the path is to raise up the true self, we cannot even begin to help you. And the one requirement for your realizing this, is that you acknowledge the fact, that you are here to raise up yourself to the 96th level. And that requires you to stop focusing on changing anyone or anything outside yourself. Is this not beginning to be clear?

You are still so identified with one of the separate spirits you have created, that you have come to the spiritual path thinking that you would get help to raise and perfect that spirit, until it becomes acceptable to God and will be allowed entry into heaven. But as Jesus said, you will not enter the wedding feast without a wedding garment. And a wedding garment is what you weave up until the 96th level of consciousness and beyond. And that, I can assure you, is a process where there is no cheating.

THE QUEST TO VALIDATE A SEPARATE SPIRIT

I understand very well, that when you look at the world and yourself through the filter of a separate spirit, you think you can get the world to conform. What is it that you are seeking to do, when you are seeking to change the world or change other people? You are seeking to get the world and other people to validate your separate self, your separate spirit. Because you think – or rather, the separate self and the ego thinks – that if the entire world acknowledges the perfection of your spirit, then God must allow it into Heaven. But you see, this is the essential illusion on the path.

When you are so identified with and blinded by this separate spirit, you think this spirit can fool God. You think you can get God and the ascended masters, including the Chohans, to look at life through the perception filter of that spirit, but it will never happen, my beloved. We will never acknowledge your perception filter as reality. Nor will we ever allow this separate spirit entry into the higher realms of our mystery schools and our etheric retreats.

We are not here to raise up the separate spirit. We are not here to raise up the unreal you. We are here to raise up the real you. This is our task. This is our love. We have infinite and unconditional love for the real you.

We also have an infinite and unconditional love for the unreal you, which is why we can see through all of its illusions. And therefore, we will not allow the separate spirits to bring their conditions into the spiritual realm, the realm of unconditionally and infinity.

I have already talked about the fact, that you are facing the journey, whereby you confront and transcend the spirits you have created, or that have been created in the collective consciousness through humankind's misuse of the seven rays. Thus, what I wish to bring to your attention today is two things: First of all, I want to reinforce what I have said earlier about the very nature of the Holy Spirit, which is that it is always flowing; it is a stream.

It is not a static spirit. It is an ever-flowing, ever-self-transcending Spirit, that never remains the same for even a split second.

The second thing is the need to keep in mind, that you are overcoming these separate spirits. And as I have said before, this will for some mean that they build a new self, a new spirit. And there is no way around this between the 48th and the 96th level of consciousness, for this is indeed your charge: to experiment with your co-creative abilities, to experiment with the seven rays, and to build a self that has some mastery of the seven rays. Nevertheless, what I would like you to keep in mind is that you are not building a self that is static. You are building a self that can flow with the Holy Spirit, the *Holy* Spirit.

THE FALSE PATH OF PERFECTING A SPIRIT

You see, the false teachers on this earth have attempted to come up with many clever schemes for how to cause those who are the sincere spiritual speakers – those who have risen above the 48th level, those who have not gone into duality – how they can cause those to go into a blind alley, that will stop their growth or even cause it to keep going down further and further into separation. And one of the main schemes they have come up with is these many subtle variations, that you can create a separate self, a spirit, that can actually gain entry into the spiritual realm.

You will see, when you think about this in light of what I have taught you in the previous discourses, that this is, of course, the ultimate dream of the ego, of the fallen beings, and of the separate spirits. A separate spirit is by definition mortal, but it dreams of immortality. It dreams of living up to some condition, whereby it becomes acceptable to God and therefore gains entry into the wedding feast with Christ.

But as Jesus said, "No man can ascend to heaven, save he who descended from heaven." The only being who can ascend to heaven is the Conscious You, and it can do so only when it sheds all of the snake-skins of the separate spirits, those false serpentine spirits that slither along the ground with their subtle serpentine logic, making you think that you will become as a god who can enter heaven.

So you will never be able to take these separate spirits with you, no matter how perfect they may be according to some earthly standard or another.

THE FALSE VIEW OF PERFECTION

Do you see the problem with the separate spirit? A separate spirit may indeed grow for a time. Think about this very carefully. A separate spirit may indeed be designed to grow and to expand and to, in a sense, perfect itself. Therefore, it is perfectly possible that you come into a religion or a spiritual teaching, and now you create an ideal in your mind, that if you keep applying the teaching, you will at some point have reached a state of perfection – some ultimate state – and then you will be allowed entry into heaven. Or you will reach enlightenment, or whatever the goal is defined as being.

But when it comes time to give up that self that you have created, then you are faced with the full force of the death consciousness. Because what do you now face? You face the very fact that in the collective consciousness is created this enormous conglomerate of these separate spirits, and they all do not want to die.

And so, if you have created a separate spirit as you walk the path of the seven rays, you will tie in to this fear of death. And therefore, you will have to overcome the entire momentum of death in order to give up this separate self. This is, of course, possible, for when you know you are pure awareness you can give up any self, but I tell you it is very rare that students are able to do this.

| *Part One - Teachings*

THE MOST DANGEROUS LEVEL OF THE PATH

The separate spirit is created out of this standard, this dualistic standard. It has within it, within its very design, this division between right and wrong. It believes that if it is proven wrong, something terrible will happen. But if it is proven right, something good should happen. Therefore, it believes that it can even force God to accept it by proving itself right. And it seeks to prove itself right in the only way it can: by comparing itself to others based on the standard out of which is was created. So it seeks to prove itself right by proving others wrong, by putting others down.

Basically, the hidden subconscious reasoning of the separate spirit is that, "If I can prove all other spirits wrong, then I must be right and God must accept *me*." But it is, of course, not so. So, do not approach the Chohans with the desire to prove yourself right. And be especially alert for the desire to prove others wrong.

And therefore, you are not proving yourself right in the eyes of the Chohans, for they are not in the dualistic state of consciousness. You are only proving yourself right in the eyes of the separate spirit you have created – the spirit that is based on your particular standard. Therefore, this spirit can never see anything beyond the standard. It can never see anything wrong with the standard. It can never see any of the limitations of the standard. It can never see that the standard is created by excluding certain elements of the greater picture of reality.

But you see, what happens to all of these lesser spirits is that they define a standard. And how do they define a standard? By excluding, by blocking out, some of the degrees—by labeling them as untrue, false, or evil in some way. And therefore, they create a standard that is based on excluding one or many of the 360 degrees of the circumference of what is possible to see on earth.

And when you define certain angles, certain degrees, as wrong, and therefore will not look at them, you will, by definition, have a limited, a selective, a subjective and a very biased and incomplete view of life. But beyond this, you will always be able to prove your separate self – your separate spirit – right. For you see, when you accept the very definition that certain degrees should not be looked at or are wrong, then of course you will not be able to see that the spirit, the perception filter through which you are looking at reality, is incomplete and only gives you a limited and distorted view of the totality of life.

YOU CAN ALWAYS PROVE YOURSELF "RIGHT"

Can you see that, if you are willing to exclude certain degrees on the circumference of the circle of life, then you can always prove that the self that can only encompass the remaining degrees is right? But can you also begin to see, that until you can see the entire circumference of the consciousness that is possible on earth, you are not enlightened, and you are not ready for the ascension?

And so, what will you be moving towards? Not the pole star of being, not the pole star of your I AM Presence. You will be moving towards the very sections that you have blocked out and have refused to see. And therefore, you will be moving towards the separate spirits you have created, that lie in wait to try to entrap you, like the sirens with their beguiling song. And soon you will be shipwrecked on the cliffs.

The point I have tried to get across in this book is that all of the things that you co-create at the identity, mental, and emotional levels form what I have chosen to call spirits. And these spirits then become part of your total being, part of the lower being that many people call the soul.

Thus, when you have created such a spirit, then the light from your I AM Presence – the stream of consciousness from your I AM Presence – will stream through it, and therefore you will continually be co-creating through that spirit. This does not mean that you will be co-creating a new spirit at every moment, but it means that as the stream of your awareness flows through a particular spirit, you will be reinforcing that spirit, and thus it becomes stronger and stronger.

And so the value of having this teaching is that it makes it possible for you to do what I have explained in earlier discourses, namely to walk the spiritual path in a much more conscious manner. In most previous teachings that have been released on this planet, people have been given only a partial understanding of what the spiritual path is about. And therefore, they have not had the concept I have given you, that you have in the past created these spirits, that these spirits have become part of your being, and that if you identify with the spirits, you cannot actually free yourself from them.

For as long as you are identified with a given spirit, your consciousness will stream through it. This will have two effects. As the stream of your consciousness is streaming through your spirit, you cannot at the same time see the spirit as a spirit and see it from the outside. But if you do not see it, you cannot free yourself from it. At the same time as your consciousness is streaming through this spirit, your energies are tied up in the spirit, and you are reinforcing the spirit, making it more difficult for yourself to pull your consciousness away from that spirit and look at that spirit from the outside.

SEEING A SPIRIT AS NOT BEING WHO YOU ARE

The saving grace in this scenario is what we have explained many times, that the Conscious You truly has the ability to project itself anywhere it wants. This means that you can at any time project yourself outside a given spirit, or you can pull yourself away from a given spirit, so that your self-awareness is not focused in the spirit and the stream of your consciousness is not flowing through that spirit.

Now, as I tell you this, it is obvious that you still have spirits in the sphere of your being, the sphere of your consciousness. Just hearing or reading these words will not mean that you will automatically pull away from them. But what I am telling you is that by having the concept in your mind and by accepting that concept, you can take your path to an entirely new level. Once you become conscious of the fact that these spirits exist in the sphere of your consciousness, you can consciously make a decision that you will engage in the process of pulling yourself away from identification with the spirits, so that you can indeed come to see a spirit from the outside.

And of course, the essential step to rising to a higher level of the spiritual path is to come to a point, where you do not identify yourself with the spirit that is the primary spirit that represents the level of consciousness you have right now.

REINFORCING A FALSE SPIRIT

As I have explained, there are 144 levels of consciousness on earth, and they can be seen as forming a spiral staircase, where each step of consciousness is one step on the staircase. In order to rise higher on the path, you have to move from one step to another on that staircase. And the only way to move from one step to the next is to dis-identify yourself from the spirit on any given step.

So my point for this book is to give you this teaching, so that you can begin to consciously follow this path of pulling your sense of identity away from these spirits. For it is only by doing so, that you will truly make progress.

There are indeed many spiritual people who have gone through the process of dis-identifying themselves from a spir-

| *Part One - Teachings*

it – giving up that spirit – and rising beyond it. But there are indeed quite a number of people on the spiritual path and in religious movements, who have studied a teaching, practiced a certain technique or religion, but they have not come to the point of freeing themselves from a given spirit. And thus, what has happened is very simple. Instead of transcending a certain spirit, all of the efforts they have put into their spiritual studies and practice have actually reinforced this spirit at a certain level of the spiritual path and a certain level of consciousness.

So you might see a person who, for example, found the spiritual path at the 56th level of consciousness. The person has then been practicing a certain technique diligently and has been studying spiritual teachings for perhaps many years. But the person has not actually transcended the spirit; it has not let go of that spirit of the 56th level of consciousness. What it has done instead is that it has directed its awareness through that spirit. And this means that as the person focused its awareness on the spiritual path and on studying a spiritual teaching, that person has actually educated the spirit of the 56th level, so that that spirit has supposedly and seemingly become more spiritual. This has given the person the impression that he or she has progressed spiritually, but in reality it is not the person – it is not the Conscious You – that has progressed; it is only the spirit.

And as I have tried to explain, that spirit does not need to progress spiritually, because it will never make it into Heaven. The only thing that will make it into Heaven is the Conscious You, and you will make it into the spiritual realm only when you dis-identify yourself from any of the spirits of the physical realm or, rather, the material realm, including the identity, mental, emotional and physical.

So you see, it is possible to be on this false path for a long time and to be fooled by the false teachers – and your own ego and your own spirits – into actually thinking that you are making progress towards the ultimate goal of your spiritual search. But in reality you are not making progress at all. You, the Conscious You, are standing still, for you are still identified with a certain spirit.

ALL NEGATIVE FEELINGS COME FROM SPIRITS

Now, this does not mean that you need to be discouraged and think you have wasted your efforts. For when you do dis-identify yourself from that spirit, then you can very quickly catch up to a higher level because of the efforts you made. Yet this will only happen when you dis-identify yourself from the spirit that you have educated, and you are willing to leave it behind. If you are not willing to leave it behind and let it die, then you will continue to reinforce it, and then the Conscious You that you are will not rise on the real path towards the ascension.

For where do such feelings come from? They come from whatever spirit is in your energy field, in your mind. It is not the Conscious You that feels afraid or discouraged or ashamed or proud or superior. It can only be a spirit, and that spirit was programmed with a thought matrix of feeling this way.

WHY YOU NEED A SPIRIT FOR A TIME

One of the things we have taught consistently is that your I AM Presence sent the Conscious You into embodiment on earth, because it wanted to experience the material world from the inside. And as you start the spiritual path at the 48th level, you are not yet aware that you are the Conscious You, and you are not yet able to simply be the open door – to be a clear pane of glass – without having an outer personality or individuality. So you need to have a self through which you can express yourself and integrate and interact with the physical body. And in taking on or creating this self, you are indeed creating a spirit.

| *Part One - Teachings*

This is inevitable. This is simply the process of taking incarnation. You cannot take incarnation as a new lifestream without creating one, or rather, many such spirits. This is perfectly natural and in order. But what can happen is that you can become trapped in identification with these spirits, instead of engaging in the process of letting one spirit die, ascending to the next level of consciousness, and then letting the spirit corresponding to that level die, and ascending to the next level and so on.

In other words, instead of consciously and constantly growing towards higher levels of consciousness, you are now trapped into reinforcing a certain spirit, based on the illusion that you can somehow expand or perfect that spirit, until it becomes acceptable to God. And you can thus enter the ascended state while being identified with that spirit, rather than entering the ascended state by giving up the very last ghost of any spirit in your lower being.

So you see the fundamental difference between the true inner path of self-transcendence and the false, outer path of seeking to perfect some kind of spirit, that is not a self-aware spirit that descended from above, but rather a non-self-aware spirit created here below. And as I have said, this does not mean that the spirit does not have some level of consciousness, but it does not have self-awareness, and that is why it cannot consciously transcend itself. This is the central ability of the Conscious You: the ability to consciously transcend itself.

But of course, you cannot transcend your sense of self without seeing that your sense of self is just a self, a spirit, that is not you. And so, the key to everything is to have this ability to pull yourself out of your current sense of self. You already have this ability, but you are not using it consciously. And this is indeed the key to taking your path to a higher level, and accelerating it beyond anything that you might have dreamt of before. So then, let me give you a few pointers.

So can you not see now, that what has happened is, that in the Middle East the people who have been warring with each other have created these collective spirits? And over thousands of years, they have fed their attention and their psycho-spiritual energy into these spirits, causing the spirits to grow stronger and stronger to the point, where they are often able to completely overpower the individuality of the average person.

If you take a look at individual people who have grown up in such an environment, you will see that there are many people who actually do not have an individual life. Yes, they will have certain individual characteristics, but they are so identified with what they think is their race or their religion or their ethnic group. But in reality, what they are identified with is the collective spirit, that was created a long time ago and has been reinforced for thousands of years. And their total identification with this spirit means that the spirit overpowers them to the point, where they could never even dream of stepping outside of the boundaries defined by what they think is their religion or culture. Therefore, they do not even imagine that they could be anything different – that they could be anything more – than what they have been brought up to see themselves as.

And so, you can see that many of these people can spend an entire lifetime without actually doing anything that is a truly free choice, that is a truly individual act. They spend their entire lifetime being so overpowered by the collective spirit, that they are literally serving as a cow that is being milked for energy, and the energy goes to sustaining and reinforcing this spirit.

Some of these spirits have grown so strong, that they look at human beings simply as cattle that are to be milked for their energy. And that is why the spirits will agitate people's emotions, causing them to go into clashes with other groups, so that people – in their anger and hatred – feed energy to the beast, to the spirit.

| *Part One - Teachings*
RECOGNIZING THE MORE SUBTLE SPIRITS

Now, of course, I am telling you this for a very simple reason. You are not overpowered by such a collective spirit to the point, where you are not able to make individual choices and take individual actions. If you had been overpowered by such a spirit – and they are, of course, found everywhere in the world – then you would not have been able to read this book. It really is that simple. And this should be an encouragement to you, because it shows you that you have already discovered the process of dis-identifying yourself from a certain spirit and consciously rising above it.

How can I say this? Because, surely, you grew up in a place where there is a collective spirit. Perhaps your family members were almost fully identified with it. Perhaps most people in your town, in your country, or in your culture are completely identified with such a collective spirit. But if you had been, you would not have been a spiritual person, and you would not have been open to this book and the spiritual path.

Even though I say that you are not completely overpowered by the collective spirit in your area, you should not take that to mean, that you are not affected by any spirit. Instead, be careful to realize a certain distinction. Because you are a spiritual person, you are not overpowered by the more common, collective spirits found on Earth. You are not completely identified with the collective spirit that dominated the culture in which you grew up.

Nevertheless, there are other collective spirits, that cannot as easily be identified with certain outer characteristics, such as race, religion, ethnic group, nationality, sex and so on. They are collective spirits that have managed to hide from most people, because they are not seen as spirits. And one of those spirits is what I have already described, namely the very aggressive spirit of wanting to prove other people wrong and wanting to prove yourself right. But there are many such spirits. They simply have not been recognized, because they are not associated with outer, physical characteristics, but with the more subtle emotional and mental characteristics, that most people are simply not aware of at this point in time.

Nevertheless, as a spiritual person, you may have well been affected by one or more of these spirits. In fact, for many people, they have become affected – or more affected – by such spirits by being involved with various spiritual groups. For there are indeed many of the spiritual, religious or New Age groups that you see today, that are very much tied into a collective spirit of a certain kind. So it is indeed possible that many people have actually become more tied into a collective spirit as a result of being involved with a spiritual teaching or organization.

Yet, beyond such collective spirits, there are of course the individual spirits that you have created. And, of course, even though you may have transcended some of these spirits, you still have other spirits that are affecting you.

How can I say this? I can say this because you are in embodiment on earth and you are reading this book. If you did not have any spirits that were affecting you, you would have ascended, and you and I would have been meeting face to face, and I would have had no need to give you this teaching.

FREEING YOURSELF FROM SPIRITS

Do you see, that there will be some spirit, that you are dealing with, until the very moment, when you give up the last ghost and ascend? This is simply the reality of the spiritual path on earth. Again, there is no reason to be discouraged by it or to feel in any way afraid or shameful about it. You just accept that this is the way it is, and then you make a decision to sharpen your ability to see through these spirits as quickly as possible and thereby free yourself from them.

| *Part One - Teachings*

Now, this is, of course, a process that in a sense you cannot completely be taught. We of the Chohans can help you in many ways. We will do so in the coming books, as we have already done in previous teachings. But nevertheless, it is really a process that has an individual aspect, because you are the one who must see it in your consciousness.

You can, of course, be told from the outside of a certain general spirit. You can even – if you have direct contact with a physical teacher or an ascended teacher through your intuition – you can be given a vision of how that spirit has taken on its individual form in you. And thereby, you can come to know that you are affected by a certain spirit, and you can know the characteristics of that spirit. But this is not quite the same as actually making that shift in consciousness, where now you have pulled the Conscious You outside of the spirit. Now you are seeing the spirit from the outside, and you are seeing that it is not you.

Perhaps you already know what I am talking about, and perhaps you don't. But if you don't, do not be discouraged. Simply continue to ponder it and continue to use the tools that we have given and will give, so that you can move closer and closer to the point, where you have diminished the magnetic pull of a certain spirit. And then the Conscious You naturally, effortlessly, and seemingly spontaneously, pulls itself out of that spirit.

Do you see what I am saying? It is natural for the Conscious You to be continuously moving, to be consciously looking at life from different perspectives. That is why you have been searching for the spiritual path. That is why you have found this book. Because the Conscious You is always looking for something different – something new – even if it does not know what it is looking for.

This is the natural aspect because, as we have said, the Conscious You is the I WILL BE aspect of your I AM Presence, the aspect that consciously says, "I will be this." But then, when it has experienced what it is like to be this, it will now say, "I will be that," and it will shift into something else in order to have that experience. And that is why it is natural for you to be identified with a certain spirit, and to experience life through the perception filter of that spirit for a time. But it is also natural for you not to remain in that spirit but to shift to a different perspective.

FORCING SPIRITS INTO THE OPEN

It is only by the spirit gaining enough momentum, that it can form a magnetic pull on your attention, so that it can artificially keep you focused through that spirit for any length of time. It is only by doing this, that the spirit can keep you trapped at that level over a period of time. That is why you see that a spirit, that is an aggressive spirit, will aggressively seek to keep you at that level. And once you begin to see this, you will actually be able to feel the aggressive force, as I imagine most of you, who will read this book, have felt it at various points in your life.

But instead of doing what you have been doing so far, which is running away from it, or resisting it, or perhaps even fighting it, I am asking you now to do something different. Simply say to yourself: "Ah! Here is a spirit that is hiding from me. I am going to force it to come out in the open, so that I can see it and thereby stop identifying myself with it, so that it will no longer have power over me. I am going to use the tools given to me by the Maha Chohan and the seven Chohans, so that I can flush these spirits out of their hiding places, where I can see that they are not me and therefore free myself from their influence."

Part Two

Invocations

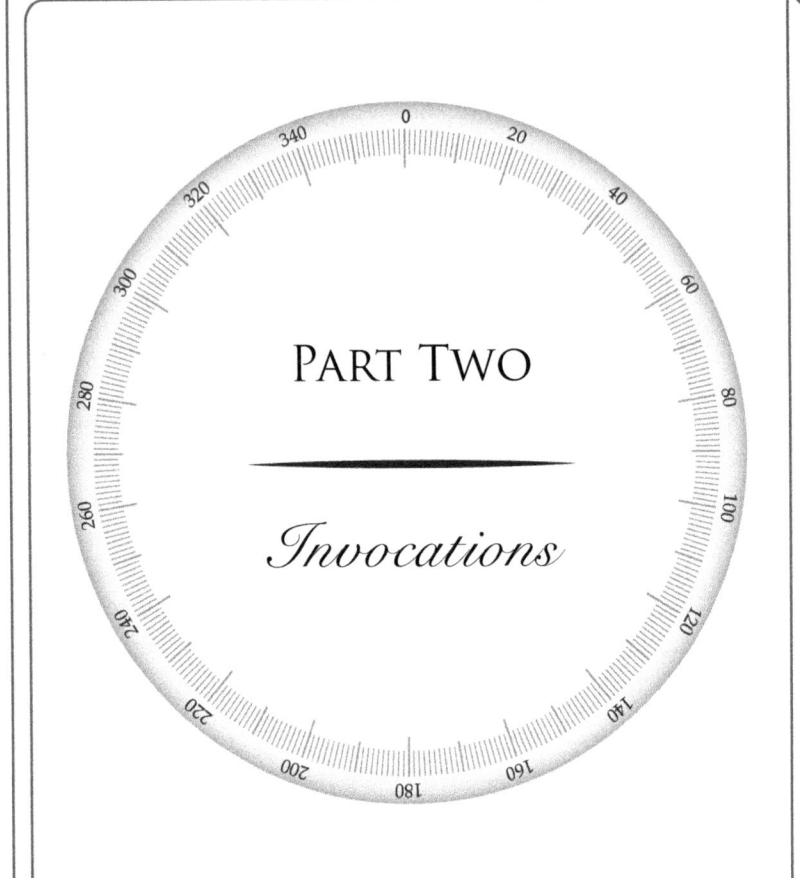

My culture, my view of life, is limited and truly
influenced by the death consciousness in subtle ways.
I do not see all of the ways in which my consciousness
is influenced by the death consciousness, but I am
beginning to see that it is influenced by the death
consciousness—and that
I want to be free of this influence.

How to give invocations

Giving an invocation is easy to do. You simply read it aloud. Obviously, if you purchased the kit with e-book and sound recordings, you can simply give the invocations along with the recordings.

Be aware that for many spiritual people, speaking an invocation aloud might require a bit of an adjustment. The reason is that many of us are so used to meditating in silence. Yet once you decide to give it a sincere try, you will likely find that you quickly get used to it. The best motivation for continuing to give invocations is that you experience that they work. You will often be amazed at how much more light you can invoke through the spoken word compared to silent meditation (not to say that silent meditation is not useful; it is simply that the spoken word is a very powerful force).

Where do I give an invocation?

You can do it anywhere, but most people prefer to sit in a private, quiet room, where they can remain undisturbed for the 25-30 minutes it takes to give a complete invocation (you can give a partial invocation if you don't have time for a full one). Most people prefer to sit in a comfortable chair. Sit in a somewhat upright, but comfortable position. It helps the energies flow better.

When do I give an invocation?

You can give an invocation any time. However, for the invocations in this book, it is probably best to give them in the evening, where you have time to contemplate the topics covered in the invocations.

| *Part Two - Invocations*

HOW DO I ACTUALLY READ THE INVOCATION?

To give an invocation, simply start reading at the beginning. An invocation always starts with an introductory paragraph that invokes specific ascended masters and sometimes describes the purpose of the invocation. After this preamble, you find words similar to these:

[Make personal calls]

At this point you can give a – short or long as you prefer – statement to dedicate the invocation to a specific purpose. For example, if you are dealing with a specific spirit that you would like to see resolved, describe it in detail and ask for the resolution of it. Don't forget to ask for the highest possible outcome—which we can't always see with our outer minds. So you might say: "In the name of the Christ, I ask for . . ." Or you might end the statement with: "In accordance with the highest vision of Christ, let it be done." Or "In accordance with God's will, let it be done." You then continue to read the invocation.

The only thing you really need to know is that all invocations are structured with a combination of specific and general – or repeated – affirmations/decrees. The specific affirmations describe specific conditions that the invocation works on. The general affirmations/decrees are repeated after the specific affirmations.

In the beginning this might seem a bit intimidating, but you will quickly get used to it, if you decide to give it a sincere try. Remember, the proof of the invocation is in the giving of it. You just can't know whether invocations work for you until you give it a try—and a sincere one.

Invocation for Transcending the Death Consciousness

In the name I AM THAT I AM, Jesus Christ, I call to my I AM Presence to flow through the I Will Be Presence that I AM and give this invocation with full power. I call to the seven Archangels and the seven Chohans, and I declare that I am willing to accelerate myself beyond the death consciousness. Therefore, I say to the Archangels and the Chohans:

Show me the way! I am willing to follow the path that you have followed and that you have proven. I am willing to follow the Path of the Seven Veils, the Path of the Seven Rays. Show me the way, and I will put one foot in front of the other and follow each direction I get, even if I do not see where it leads, even if it does not exactly correspond to my expectations. For I am beginning to realize, that my expectations are indeed very limited.

My culture, my view of life, is limited and truly influenced by the death consciousness in subtle ways. I do not see all of the ways in which my consciousness is influenced by the death consciousness, but I am beginning to see that it is influenced by the death consciousness—and that I want to be free of this influence. And I know that I am only able to be free by having a frame of reference from beings, that have already accelerated themselves beyond it. That is why I am willing to follow you, the Archangels and the Chohans. So show me the next step, and I will take that next step. Help me especially see and overcome the following aspect of the death consciousness:

[Make personal calls]

God is Father and Mother
God is Father, God is Mother,
never one without the other.

Your balanced union is our source,
your Love will keep us on our course.
You offer us abundant life,
to free us from all sense of strife.
We plunge ourselves into the stream,
awakening from this bad dream.
We see that life is truly one,
and thus our victory is won.
We have returned unto our God,
on the path the saints have trod.
We form God's body on the Earth,
and give our planet its rebirth,
into a Golden Age of Love,
with ample blessings from Above.
We set all people free to see
that oneness is reality,
and in that oneness we will be
whole for all eternity.
And now the Earth is truly healed,
all life in God's perfection sealed.

God is Father, God is Mother,
we see God in each other.

1st Ray

1. Archangel Michael, consume in my entire being the perverted power of the death consciousness, especially the aggressive force that wants me to react, to engage or even seek to fight or destroy it.

Michael Archangel, in your flame so blue,
there is no more night, there is only you.
In oneness with you, I am filled with your light,
what glorious wonder, revealed to my sight.

**Michael Archangel, your Faith is so strong,
Michael Archangel, oh sweep me along.
Michael Archangel, I'm singing your song,
Michael Archangel, with you I belong.**

2. Archangel Michael, consume in my entire being the perverted power of the death consciousness, especially the force that seeks to cover over, camouflage or misdirect my inner knowing that life is an ongoing process.

Michael Archangel, protection you give,
within your blue shield, I ever shall live.
Sealed from all creatures, roaming the night,
I remain in your sphere, of electric blue light.

**Michael Archangel, your Faith is so strong,
Michael Archangel, oh sweep me along.
Michael Archangel, I'm singing your song,
Michael Archangel, with you I belong.**

3. Archangel Michael, consume in my entire being the perverted power of the death consciousness, especially all expectations of what life should be like, where it should be going and what is the ultimate goal.

Michael Archangel, what power you bring,
as millions of angels, praises will sing.
Consuming the demons, of doubt and of fear,
I know that your Presence, will always be near.

**Michael Archangel, your Faith is so strong,
Michael Archangel, oh sweep me along.
Michael Archangel, I'm singing your song,
Michael Archangel, with you I belong.**

| *Part Two - Invocations*

4. Archangel Michael, consume in my entire being the perverted power of the death consciousness, especially all resistance to the ongoingness of the River of Life.

Michael Archangel, God's will is your love,
you bring to us all, God's light from Above.
God's will is to see, all life taking flight,
transcendence of self, our most sacred right.

Michael Archangel, your Faith is so strong,
Michael Archangel, oh sweep me along.
Michael Archangel, I'm singing your song,
Michael Archangel, with you I belong.

5. Archangel Michael, consume in my entire being the perverted power of the death consciousness, especially all desire to own, possess or control anything in this world.

With angels I soar,
as I reach for MORE.
The angels so real,
their love all will heal.
The angels bring peace,
all conflicts will cease.
With angels of light,
we soar to new height.

The rustling sound of angel wings,
what joy as even matter sings,
what joy as every atom rings,
in harmony with angel wings.

2nd Ray

1. Archangel Jophiel, consume in my entire being the false wisdom of the death consciousness, especially the force that wants me to judge, analyze and evaluate everything that is going on around me.

Jophiel Archangel, in wisdom's great light,
all serpentine lies exposed to my sight.
So subtle the lies that creep through the mind,
yet you are the greatest teacher I find.

Jophiel Archangel, exposing all lies,
Jophiel Archangel, cutting all ties.
Jophiel Archangel, clearing the skies,
Jophiel Archangel, my mind truly flies.

2. Archangel Jophiel, consume in my entire being the false wisdom of the death consciousness, especially the force that wants me to be constantly evaluating myself and every aspect of my life.

Jophiel Archangel, your wisdom I hail,
your sword cutting through duality's veil.
As you show the way, I know what is real,
from serpentine doubt, I instantly heal.

Jophiel Archangel, exposing all lies,
Jophiel Archangel, cutting all ties.
Jophiel Archangel, clearing the skies,
Jophiel Archangel, my mind truly flies.

3. Archangel Jophiel, consume in my entire being the false wisdom of the death consciousness, especially the standard for what it means to be a good human being, and the force that wants me to conform to this standard.

> Jophiel Archangel, your reality,
> the best antidote to duality.
> No lie can remain in your Presence so clear,
> with you on my side, no serpent I fear.
>
> **Jophiel Archangel, exposing all lies,**
> **Jophiel Archangel, cutting all ties.**
> **Jophiel Archangel, clearing the skies,**
> **Jophiel Archangel, my mind truly flies.**

4. Archangel Jophiel, consume in my entire being the false wisdom of the death consciousness, especially the lies of the false hierarchy of fallen beings, who use the subtleties of the death consciousness to enslave and control me.

> Jophiel Archangel, God's mind is in me,
> and through your clear light, its wisdom I see.
> Divisions all vanish, as I see the One,
> and truly, the wholeness of mind I have won.
>
> **Jophiel Archangel, exposing all lies,**
> **Jophiel Archangel, cutting all ties.**
> **Jophiel Archangel, clearing the skies,**
> **Jophiel Archangel, my mind truly flies.**

5. Archangel Jophiel, consume in my entire being the false wisdom of the death consciousness, and help me see the many subtle ways in which I have been influenced by it.

With angels I soar,
as I reach for MORE.
The angels so real,
their love all will heal.
The angels bring peace,
all conflicts will cease.
With angels of light,
we soar to new height.

The rustling sound of angel wings,
what joy as even matter sings,
what joy as every atom rings,
in harmony with angel wings.

3rd Ray

1. Archangel Chamuel, consume in my entire being the conditional love of the death consciousness, and help me see how this aggressive force has camouflaged itself, so that I don't even see its influence.

Chamuel Archangel, in ruby ray power,
I know I am taking a life-giving shower.
Love burning away all perversions of will,
I suddenly feel my desires falling still.

Chamuel Archangel, descend from Above,
Chamuel Archangel, with ruby-pink love,
Chamuel Archangel, so often thought-of,
Chamuel Archangel, o come Holy Dove.

| *Part Two - Invocations*

2. Archangel Chamuel, consume in my entire being the conditional love of the death consciousness, and help me truly experience the Divine Love, that is the ultimate frame of reference from outside the illusions of the death consciousness.

> Chamuel Archangel, a spiral of light,
> as ruby ray fire now pierces the night.
> All forces of darkness consumed by your fire,
> consuming all those who will not rise higher.
>
> **Chamuel Archangel, descend from Above,**
> **Chamuel Archangel, with ruby-pink love,**
> **Chamuel Archangel, so often thought-of,**
> **Chamuel Archangel, o come Holy Dove.**

3. Archangel Chamuel, consume in my entire being the conditional love of the death consciousness, for I am willing to rise beyond my normal state of consciousness and truly experience, that there is MORE than the death consciousness.

> Chamuel Archangel, your love so immense,
> with clarified vision, my life now makes sense.
> The purpose of life you so clearly reveal,
> immersed in your love, God's oneness I feel.
>
> **Chamuel Archangel, descend from Above,**
> **Chamuel Archangel, with ruby-pink love,**
> **Chamuel Archangel, so often thought-of,**
> **Chamuel Archangel, o come Holy Dove.**

4. Archangel Chamuel, consume in my entire being the conditional love of the death consciousness, so I can know that I am MORE than the death consciousness.

> Chamuel Archangel, what calmness you bring,
> I see now that even death has no sting.
> For truly, in love there can be no decay,
> as love is transcendence into a new day.

Chamuel Archangel, descend from Above,
Chamuel Archangel, with ruby-pink love,
Chamuel Archangel, so often thought-of,
Chamuel Archangel, o come Holy Dove.

5. Archangel Chamuel, consume in my entire being the conditional love of the death consciousness, for I know I am more and I refuse to conform to the death consciousness.

> With angels I soar,
> as I reach for MORE.
> The angels so real,
> their love all will heal.
> The angels bring peace,
> all conflicts will cease.
> With angels of light,
> we soar to new height.

The rustling sound of angel wings,
what joy as even matter sings,
what joy as every atom rings,
in harmony with angel wings.

| *Part Two - Invocations*

4th Ray

1. Archangel Gabriel, consume in my entire being the impure vibrations of the death consciousness, and help me accelerate myself beyond the closed system of my outer mind.

> Gabriel Archangel, your light I revere,
> immersed in your Presence, nothing I fear.
> A disciple of Christ, I do leave behind,
> the ego's desire for responding in kind.
>
> **Gabriel Archangel, of this I am sure,**
> **Gabriel Archangel, Christ light is the cure.**
> **Gabriel Archangel, intentions so pure,**
> **Gabriel Archangel, in you I'm secure.**

2. Archangel Gabriel, consume in my entire being the impure vibrations of the death consciousness, for I am willing to immerse myself completely in the flow of the River of Life.

> Gabriel Archangel, I fear not the light,
> in purifications' fire, I delight.
> With your hand in mine, each challenge I face,
> I follow the spiral to infinite grace.
>
> **Gabriel Archangel, of this I am sure,**
> **Gabriel Archangel, Christ light is the cure.**
> **Gabriel Archangel, intentions so pure,**
> **Gabriel Archangel, in you I'm secure.**

3. Archangel Gabriel, consume in my entire being the impure vibrations of the death consciousness, for I am willing to accelerate beyond the closed system in which my ego feels comfortable.

> Gabriel Archangel, your fire burning white,
> ascending with you, out of the night.
> My ego has nowhere to run and to hide,
> in ascension's bright spiral, with you I abide.
>
> **Gabriel Archangel, of this I am sure,**
> **Gabriel Archangel, Christ light is the cure.**
> **Gabriel Archangel, intentions so pure,**
> **Gabriel Archangel, in you I'm secure.**

4. Archangel Gabriel, consume in my entire being the impure vibrations of the death consciousness, for I am willing to accelerate beyond the closed system and the downward spiral of the ego.

> Gabriel Archangel, your trumpet I hear,
> announcing the birth of Christ drawing near.
> In lightness of being, I now am reborn,
> rising with Christ on bright Easter morn.
>
> **Gabriel Archangel, of this I am sure,**
> **Gabriel Archangel, Christ light is the cure.**
> **Gabriel Archangel, intentions so pure,**
> **Gabriel Archangel, in you I'm secure.**

| *Part Two - Invocations*

5. Archangel Gabriel, consume in my entire being the impure vibrations of the death consciousness, especially the spiral of the death consciousness becoming increasingly extreme, until something breaks down.

> With angels I soar,
> as I reach for MORE.
> The angels so real,
> their love all will heal.
> The angels bring peace,
> all conflicts will cease.
> With angels of light,
> we soar to new height.
>
> **The rustling sound of angel wings,**
> **what joy as even matter sings,**
> **what joy as every atom rings,**
> **in harmony with angel wings.**

5th Ray

1. Archangel Raphael, consume in my entire being the dualistic vision of the death consciousness, for I am willing to step onto the true path; I am willing to accelerate my state of consciousness beyond death.

> Raphael Archangel, your light so intense,
> raise me beyond all human pretense.
> Mother Mary and you have a vision so bold,
> to see that our highest potential unfold.
>
> **Raphael Archangel, for vision I pray,**
> **Raphael Archangel, show me the way,**
> **Raphael Archangel, your emerald ray,**
> **Raphael Archangel, my life a new day.**

2. Archangel Raphael, consume in my entire being the dualistic vision of the death consciousness, for I am willing to look at my perception filter and attain true vision.

> Raphael Archangel, in emerald sphere,
> to immaculate vision I always adhere.
> Mother Mary enfolds me in her sacred heart,
> from Mother's true love, I am never apart.

> **Raphael Archangel, for vision I pray,**
> **Raphael Archangel, show me the way,**
> **Raphael Archangel, your emerald ray,**
> **Raphael Archangel, my life a new day.**

3. Archangel Raphael, consume in my entire being the dualistic vision of the death consciousness, for I am willing to have you challenge my expectations, my comfortability and all aspects of the death consciousness in my being and world.

> Raphael Archangel, all ailments you heal,
> each cell in my body in light now you seal.
> Mother Mary's immaculate concept I see,
> perfection of health is real now for me.

> **Raphael Archangel, for vision I pray,**
> **Raphael Archangel, show me the way,**
> **Raphael Archangel, your emerald ray,**
> **Raphael Archangel, my life a new day.**

| *Part Two - Invocations*

4. Archangel Raphael, consume in my entire being the dualistic vision of the death consciousness, for I am willing to experience the vibration of the ascended masters, I am willing to attune my consciousness to your vibration as the priceless opportunity to grow.

> Raphael Archangel, your light is so real,
> the vision of Christ in me you reveal.
> Mother Mary now helps me to truly transcend,
> in emerald light with you I ascend.
>
> **Raphael Archangel, for vision I pray,**
> **Raphael Archangel, show me the way,**
> **Raphael Archangel, your emerald ray,**
> **Raphael Archangel, my life a new day.**

5. Archangel Raphael, consume in my entire being the dualistic vision of the death consciousness, especially all denial, fear and guilt that can prevent me from truly seeing the death consciousness in myself.

> With angels I soar,
> as I reach for MORE.
> The angels so real,
> their love all will heal.
> The angels bring peace,
> all conflicts will cease.
> With angels of light,
> we soar to new height.
>
> **The rustling sound of angel wings,**
> **what joy as even matter sings,**
> **what joy as every atom rings,**
> **in harmony with angel wings.**

6th Ray

1. Archangel Uriel, consume in my entire being the anti-peace of the death consciousness, especially the fear of something bad happening to me, including the fear of war or calamities.

> Uriel Archangel, immense is the power,
> of angels of peace, all war to devour.
> The demons of war, no match for your light,
> consuming them all, with radiance so bright.
>
> **Uriel Archangel, use your great sword,**
> **Uriel Archangel, consume all discord,**
> **Uriel Archangel, we're of one accord,**
> **Uriel Archangel, we walk with the Lord.**

2. Archangel Uriel, consume in my entire being the anti-peace of the death consciousness, especially the force that wants me to think I am better than others, and wants to put others down or prove them wrong.

> Uriel Archangel, intense is the sound,
> when millions of angels, their voices compound.
> They build a crescendo, piercing the night,
> life's glorious oneness revealed to our sight.
>
> **Uriel Archangel, use your great sword,**
> **Uriel Archangel, consume all discord,**
> **Uriel Archangel, we're of one accord,**
> **Uriel Archangel, we walk with the Lord.**

| *Part Two - Invocations*

3. Archangel Uriel, consume in my entire being the anti-peace of the death consciousness, especially the feeling that I have to compensate for something, that I have to justify my ego.

> Uriel Archangel, from out the Great Throne,
> your millions of trumpets, sound the One Tone.
> Consuming all discord with your harmony,
> the sound of all sounds will set all life free.
>
> **Uriel Archangel, use your great sword,**
> **Uriel Archangel, consume all discord,**
> **Uriel Archangel, we're of one accord,**
> **Uriel Archangel, we walk with the Lord.**

4. Archangel Uriel, consume in my entire being the anti-peace of the death consciousness, especially the feeling of being threatened, causing me to project out in an attempt to control others and hold them back.

> Uriel Archangel, all war is now gone,
> for you bring a message, from heart of the One
> The hearts of all men, now singing in peace,
> the spirals of love, forever increase.
>
> **Uriel Archangel, use your great sword,**
> **Uriel Archangel, consume all discord,**
> **Uriel Archangel, we're of one accord,**
> **Uriel Archangel, we walk with the Lord.**

5. Archangel Uriel, consume in my entire being the anti-peace of the death consciousness, especially all desire to prove people or ideas wrong, to have them humiliated, exposed or put down.

> With angels I soar,
> as I reach for MORE.
> The angels so real,
> their love all will heal.

The angels bring peace,
all conflicts will cease.
With angels of light,
we soar to new height.

The rustling sound of angel wings,
what joy as even matter sings,
what joy as every atom rings,
in harmony with angel wings.

7th Ray

1. Archangel Zadkiel, consume in my entire being the anti-freedom of the death consciousness, especially the subtle aggressive force, which plays on my emotions. Consume the constant projection that tries to agitate me into emotions that are based on fear and not on love.

Zadkiel Archangel, your flow is so swift,
in your violet light, I instantly shift,
into a vibration in which I am free,
from all limitations of the lesser me.

Zadkiel Archangel, encircle the earth,
Zadkiel Archangel, with your violet girth,
Zadkiel Archangel, unstoppable mirth,
Zadkiel Archangel, our planet's rebirth.

| *Part Two - Invocations*

2. Archangel Zadkiel, consume in my entire being the anti-freedom of the death consciousness, especially the constant projection on my mental body, seeking to force my thoughts into patterns that form closed loops, where the mind goes round and round, because the ego is projecting that the change needs to happen out there.

> Zadkiel Archangel, I truly aspire,
> to being the master of your violet fire.
> Wielding the power, of your alchemy,
> I use Sacred Word, to set all life free.

> **Zadkiel Archangel, encircle the earth,**
> **Zadkiel Archangel, with your violet girth,**
> **Zadkiel Archangel, unstoppable mirth,**
> **Zadkiel Archangel, our planet's rebirth.**

3. Archangel Zadkiel, consume in my entire being the anti-freedom of the death consciousness, especially what makes me think I can overcome the death consciousness by using the death consciousness.

> Zadkiel Archangel, your violet light,
> transforming the earth, with unstoppable might.
> So swiftly our planet, beginning to spin,
> with legions of angels, our victory we win.

> **Zadkiel Archangel, encircle the earth,**
> **Zadkiel Archangel, with your violet girth,**
> **Zadkiel Archangel, unstoppable mirth,**
> **Zadkiel Archangel, our planet's rebirth.**

4. Archangel Zadkiel, consume in my entire being the anti-freedom of the death consciousness, especially the illusions that take away my freedom, because I have no frame of reference from outside the death consciousness.

> Zadkiel Archangel, your violet flame,
> the earth and humanity, never the same.
> Saint Germain's Golden Age, is a reality,
> what glorious wonder, I joyously see.

> **Zadkiel Archangel, encircle the earth,**
> **Zadkiel Archangel, with your violet girth,**
> **Zadkiel Archangel, unstoppable mirth,**
> **Zadkiel Archangel, our planet's rebirth.**

5. Archangel Zadkiel, consume in my entire being the anti-freedom of the death consciousness, for I am willing to look at and look beyond any aspect of my perception filter, that stands in the way of my experiencing myself as the pure awareness, which makes me an open door for my I AM Presence.

> With angels I soar,
> as I reach for MORE.
> The angels so real,
> their love all will heal.
> The angels bring peace,
> all conflicts will cease.
> With angels of light,
> we soar to new height.

> **The rustling sound of angel wings,**
> **what joy as even matter sings,**
> **what joy as every atom rings,**
> **in harmony with angel wings.**

Oneness Decree

In the name of the I AM THAT I AM, Jesus Christ, I acknowledge that I have in various ways submitted to the death consciousness and that this has caused me to separate myself from the River of Life. Yet I also declare that I am willing to come apart from the death consciousness and plunge myself into the oneness of the River of life. Thus, I say:

Maha Chohan, seven Chohans, show me the way. I am willing to rise beyond the death consciousness. I realize I cannot see right now how I have been influenced by the death consciousness. I want you to teach me. I want you to show me. I want to come up higher. And I am willing to look at myself and look at my expectations and my mental images and my perception filter. And I am willing to have you challenge it. I may not be able to have you challenge it all at once, but I am willing to have it challenged in bits and pieces, so that I can gradually come up higher while maintaining some sense of continuity of who I am. To this end I decree:

1. Surya, thou perfectly balanced one,
shining your light like a radiant sun,
from the God Star infusing the Earth
with unstoppable power, producing rebirth.

**Oh Alpha-Omega in Great Central Sun,
release now the Infinite Power of One,
to shatter the veil of duality's lies,
cutting all people free from its ties.**

**Beloved Surya, your balancing power,
flooding the Earth like a radiant shower,
as Father and Mother in oneness we see,
in infinite bliss forever we'll be.**

2. Resurrecting the feminine in woman and man,
revealing the matrix of God's perfect plan,

consuming all images graven and old,
raising religion beyond earthly mold.

**Oh Alpha-Omega in Great Central Sun,
release now the Infinite Power of One,
to shatter the veil of duality's lies,
cutting all people free from its ties.**

**Beloved Surya, your balancing power,
flooding the Earth like a radiant shower,
as Father and Mother in oneness we see,
in infinite bliss forever we'll be.**

3. Saint Germain's Golden Age a reality at last,
the lies of duality a thing of the past,
the Mother Divine is raised up in all,
who listen within and follow the call.

**Oh Alpha-Omega in Great Central Sun,
release now the Infinite Power of One,
to shatter the veil of duality's lies,
cutting all people free from its ties.**

**Beloved Surya, your balancing power,
flooding the Earth like a radiant shower,
as Father and Mother in oneness we see,
in infinite bliss forever we'll be.**

4. Maraytaii is the name of the Mother Divine,
who calls all her children to let their light shine,
with Jesus we now take the ultimate stand,
affirming the Kingdom of God is at hand.

**Oh Alpha-Omega in Great Central Sun,
release now the Infinite Power of One,
to shatter the veil of duality's lies,
cutting all people free from its ties.**

**Beloved Surya, your balancing power,
flooding the Earth like a radiant shower,
as Father and Mother in oneness we see,
in infinite bliss forever we'll be.**

5. Mother Mary is showing all people the way,
to the kingdom within through the feminine ray,
for when we see God within every form,
we know that abundance is truly the norm.

**Oh Alpha-Omega in Great Central Sun,
release now the Infinite Power of One,
to shatter the veil of duality's lies,
cutting all people free from its ties.**

**Beloved Surya, your balancing power,
flooding the Earth like a radiant shower,
as Father and Mother in oneness we see,
in infinite bliss forever we'll be.**

6. And now we are led by the great Master MORE,
across the vast sea to a welcoming shore,
where all of duality's voices will cease,
as with the Lord Buddha we're centered in peace.

**Oh Alpha-Omega in Great Central Sun,
release now the Infinite Power of One,
to shatter the veil of duality's lies,
cutting all people free from its ties.**

**Beloved Surya, your balancing power,
flooding the Earth like a radiant shower,
as Father and Mother in oneness we see,
in infinite bliss forever we'll be.**

7. As Alpha-Omega their union reveal,
we know separation cannot be real,
and thus we can enter the Great Central Sun,
where ultimate victory of union is won.

**Oh Alpha-Omega in Great Central Sun,
release now the Infinite Power of One,
to shatter the veil of duality's lies,
cutting all people free from its ties.**

**Beloved Surya, your balancing power,
flooding the Earth like a radiant shower,
as Father and Mother in oneness we see,
in infinite bliss forever we'll be.**

8. And thus we go forth to proclaim the great plan,
to bridge separation between God and Man.
Accepting the call co-creators to be,
as we raise the Earth to her God-victory.

**Oh Alpha-Omega in Great Central Sun,
release now the Infinite Power of One,
to shatter the veil of duality's lies,
cutting all people free from its ties.**

**Beloved Surya, your balancing power,
flooding the Earth like a radiant shower,
as Father and Mother in oneness we see,
in infinite bliss forever we'll be.**

Sealing:

In the name of the Divine Mother, I call to the seven Archangels for the protection and sealing of myself and all people in my circle of influence from any backlash from the forces of the death consciousness. I call for the multiplication of my calls by the entire Spirit of the Ascended Masters, so that we form the perfect figure-eight flow of "As Above, so below." Thus, I accept that this is fully manifest, because the mouth of the Lord, the Christ within me, has spoken it. Amen.

Invocation for Freedom from Aggressive Spirits

In the name I AM THAT I AM, Jesus Christ, I call to my I AM Presence to flow through the I Will Be Presence that I AM and give this invocation with full power. I call to the seven Archangels to protect me and cut me free from all aggressive and false spirits seeking to limit my creative freedom and my ability to rise to the next level of my spiritual path, including…

[Make personal calls]

God is Father and Mother
God is Father, God is Mother,
never one without the other.

Your balanced union is our source,
your Love will keep us on our course.
You offer us abundant life,
to free us from all sense of strife.
We plunge ourselves into the stream,
awakening from this bad dream.
We see that life is truly one,
and thus our victory is won.
We have returned unto our God,
on the path the saints have trod.
We form God's body on the Earth,
and give our planet its rebirth,
into a Golden Age of Love,
with ample blessings from Above.
We set all people free to see
that oneness is reality,
and in that oneness we will be
whole for all eternity.

And now the Earth is truly healed,
all life in God's perfection sealed.

God is Father, God is Mother,
we see God in each other.

1st Ray

1. Archangel Michael, place an impenetrable shield of blue flame protection around my entire being, sealing me from the influence of all aggressive spirits in the four levels of the material realm.

Michael Archangel, in your flame so blue,
there is no more night, there is only you.
In oneness with you, I am filled with your light,
what glorious wonder, revealed to my sight.

Michael Archangel, your Faith is so strong,
Michael Archangel, oh sweep me along.
Michael Archangel, I'm singing your song,
Michael Archangel, with you I belong.

2. Archangel Michael, let your shield of blue flame protection form an impenetrable shield, so that no aggressive spirits in my own being can influence other people.

Michael Archangel, protection you give,
within your blue shield, I ever shall live.
Sealed from all creatures, roaming the night,
I remain in your sphere, of electric blue light.

Michael Archangel, your Faith is so strong,
Michael Archangel, oh sweep me along.
Michael Archangel, I'm singing your song,
Michael Archangel, with you I belong.

3. Archangel Michael, bind all aggressive spirits in my own being and expose to me the one I need to deal with right now. For I am willing to look into my subconscious mind and see the spirit that is preventing me from taking the next step on my path.

> Michael Archangel, what power you bring,
> as millions of angels, praises will sing.
> Consuming the demons, of doubt and of fear,
> I know that your Presence, will always be near.
>
> **Michael Archangel, your Faith is so strong,**
> **Michael Archangel, oh sweep me along.**
> **Michael Archangel, I'm singing your song,**
> **Michael Archangel, with you I belong.**

4. Archangel Michael, protect and seal me from all aggressive spirits that seek to steal light from me through physical or psychic force.

> Michael Archangel, God's will is your love,
> you bring to us all, God's light from Above.
> God's will is to see, all life taking flight,
> transcendence of self, our most sacred right.
>
> **Michael Archangel, your Faith is so strong,**
> **Michael Archangel, oh sweep me along.**
> **Michael Archangel, I'm singing your song,**
> **Michael Archangel, with you I belong.**

5. Archangel Michael, bind all aggressive spirits in my own being that seek to steal light from other people through physical or psychic force. I now see that I can get light directly from the spiritual realm, so I do not need to get energy from this realm.

> With angels I soar,
> as I reach for MORE.
> The angels so real,
> their love all will heal.
> The angels bring peace,
> all conflicts will cease.
> With angels of light,
> we soar to new height.

The rustling sound of angel wings,
what joy as even matter sings,
what joy as every atom rings,
in harmony with angel wings.

2nd Ray

1. Archangel Jophiel, protect and seal me from all aggressive spirits that seek to steal light from me through deceit, fooling me into giving them light.

> Jophiel Archangel, in wisdom's great light,
> all serpentine lies exposed to my sight.
> So subtle the lies that creep through the mind,
> yet you are the greatest teacher I find.

Jophiel Archangel, exposing all lies,
Jophiel Archangel, cutting all ties.
Jophiel Archangel, clearing the skies,
Jophiel Archangel, my mind truly flies.

| *Part Two - Invocations*

2. Archangel Jophiel, shatter the veil of illusion created by the deceptive spirits in my being, so that I can see the spirit that is right now aggressively taking energy from myself and other people.

> Jophiel Archangel, your wisdom I hail,
> your sword cutting through duality's veil.
> As you show the way, I know what is real,
> from serpentine doubt, I instantly heal.
>
> **Jophiel Archangel, exposing all lies,**
> **Jophiel Archangel, cutting all ties.**
> **Jophiel Archangel, clearing the skies,**
> **Jophiel Archangel, my mind truly flies.**

3. Archangel Jophiel, bind all spirits in my being that aggressively project their thought matrix upon me or upon other people through me. Help me see the spirit that is attacking me right now.

> Jophiel Archangel, your reality,
> the best antidote to duality.
> No lie can remain in your Presence so clear,
> with you on my side, no serpent I fear.
>
> **Jophiel Archangel, exposing all lies,**
> **Jophiel Archangel, cutting all ties.**
> **Jophiel Archangel, clearing the skies,**
> **Jophiel Archangel, my mind truly flies.**

4. Archangel Jophiel, shatter the veil of illusion, so that I can see the false spirit that corresponds to my present level of consciousness and how it is seeking to prevent me from rising to the next level.

> Jophiel Archangel, God's mind is in me,
> and through your clear light, its wisdom I see.
> Divisions all vanish, as I see the One,
> and truly, the wholeness of mind I have won.
>
> **Jophiel Archangel, exposing all lies,**
> **Jophiel Archangel, cutting all ties.**
> **Jophiel Archangel, clearing the skies,**
> **Jophiel Archangel, my mind truly flies.**

5. Archangel Jophiel, shatter the veil of illusion, so that I can see both the spirit I have created at my current level of consciousness and the corresponding false spirit that seeks to pull me below the 48th level of awareness.

> With angels I soar,
> as I reach for MORE.
> The angels so real,
> their love all will heal.
> The angels bring peace,
> all conflicts will cease.
> With angels of light,
> we soar to new height.
>
> **The rustling sound of angel wings,**
> **what joy as even matter sings,**
> **what joy as every atom rings,**
> **in harmony with angel wings.**

| Part Two - Invocations

3rd Ray

1. Archangel Chamuel, bind all dead spirits in my being, the spirits that move further away from oneness for each time they seek to get energy from others.

> Chamuel Archangel, in ruby ray power,
> I know I am taking a life-giving shower.
> Love burning away all perversions of will,
> I suddenly feel my desires falling still.
>
> **Chamuel Archangel, descend from Above,**
> **Chamuel Archangel, with ruby-pink love,**
> **Chamuel Archangel, so often thought-of,**
> **Chamuel Archangel, o come Holy Dove.**

2. Archangel Chamuel, shatter the veil of anti-love in my being, so that I can experience the true love I have for God, the love that pulls me closer to oneness.

> Chamuel Archangel, a spiral of light,
> as ruby ray fire now pierces the night.
> All forces of darkness consumed by your fire,
> consuming all those who will not rise higher.
>
> **Chamuel Archangel, descend from Above,**
> **Chamuel Archangel, with ruby-pink love,**
> **Chamuel Archangel, so often thought-of,**
> **Chamuel Archangel, o come Holy Dove.**

3. Archangel Chamuel, shatter the veil of anti-love, so I can see and surrender the aggressive spirit that is seeking to pull me into the dualistic struggle against some kind of opponent.

> Chamuel Archangel, your love so immense,
> with clarified vision, my life now makes sense.
> The purpose of life you so clearly reveal,
> immersed in your love, God's oneness I feel.

> **Chamuel Archangel, descend from Above,**
> **Chamuel Archangel, with ruby-pink love,**
> **Chamuel Archangel, so often thought-of,**
> **Chamuel Archangel, o come Holy Dove.**

4. Archangel Chamuel, shatter the veil of anti-love, so I can see and surrender the aggressive spirit that is seeking to justify why I do not transcend my current level, but stay where my ego feels comfortable.

> Chamuel Archangel, what calmness you bring,
> I see now that even death has no sting.
> For truly, in love there can be no decay,
> as love is transcendence into a new day.

> **Chamuel Archangel, descend from Above,**
> **Chamuel Archangel, with ruby-pink love,**
> **Chamuel Archangel, so often thought-of,**
> **Chamuel Archangel, o come Holy Dove.**

| *Part Two - Invocations*

5. Archangel Chamuel, shatter the veil of anti-love, so I can see and surrender the spirit behind the epic mindset of thinking I have to engage in some ultimate battle between good and evil. I now see the higher love that calls on me to leave the dualistic struggle behind and move closer to oneness.

> With angels I soar,
> as I reach for MORE.
> The angels so real,
> their love all will heal.
> The angels bring peace,
> all conflicts will cease.
> With angels of light,
> we soar to new height.

> **The rustling sound of angel wings,**
> **what joy as even matter sings,**
> **what joy as every atom rings,**
> **in harmony with angel wings.**

4th Ray

1. Archangel Gabriel, accelerate my entire energy field, so I can rise to the determination to slay all aggressive spirits in my being and thereby make my personal contribution to raising the collective consciousness.

> Gabriel Archangel, your light I revere,
> immersed in your Presence, nothing I fear.
> A disciple of Christ, I do leave behind,
> the ego's desire for responding in kind.

> **Gabriel Archangel, of this I am sure,**
> **Gabriel Archangel, Christ light is the cure.**
> **Gabriel Archangel, intentions so pure,**
> **Gabriel Archangel, in you I'm secure.**

2. Archangel Gabriel, bind the spirit within my being that cannot stand my current situation. Help me accelerate my consciousness, so I can see the way out of the catch-22 created by the spirit that is holding me back.

> Gabriel Archangel, I fear not the light,
> in purifications' fire, I delight.
> With your hand in mine, each challenge I face,
> I follow the spiral to infinite grace.

> **Gabriel Archangel, of this I am sure,**
> **Gabriel Archangel, Christ light is the cure.**
> **Gabriel Archangel, intentions so pure,**
> **Gabriel Archangel, in you I'm secure.**

3. Archangel Gabriel, accelerate my consciousness, so I can experience myself as pure awareness, thus knowing that I have only created a spirit; I have not become that spirit.

> Gabriel Archangel, your fire burning white,
> ascending with you, out of the night.
> My ego has nowhere to run and to hide,
> in ascension's bright spiral, with you I abide.

> **Gabriel Archangel, of this I am sure,**
> **Gabriel Archangel, Christ light is the cure.**
> **Gabriel Archangel, intentions so pure,**
> **Gabriel Archangel, in you I'm secure.**

4. Archangel Gabriel, accelerate my consciousness, so I can see and transcend the negative, aggressive spirit that corresponds to my current level of consciousness.

> Gabriel Archangel, your trumpet I hear,
> announcing the birth of Christ drawing near.
> In lightness of being, I now am reborn,
> rising with Christ on bright Easter morn.

Part Two - Invocations

> **Gabriel Archangel, of this I am sure,**
> **Gabriel Archangel, Christ light is the cure.**
> **Gabriel Archangel, intentions so pure,**
> **Gabriel Archangel, in you I'm secure.**

5. Archangel Gabriel, accelerate my consciousness, so I can see that the only way to grow is to see the spirit of my current level of consciousness and then consciously decide to let that spirit die.

> With angels I soar,
> as I reach for MORE.
> The angels so real,
> their love all will heal.
> The angels bring peace,
> all conflicts will cease.
> With angels of light,
> we soar to new height.

> **The rustling sound of angel wings,**
> **what joy as even matter sings,**
> **what joy as every atom rings,**
> **in harmony with angel wings.**

5th Ray

1. Archangel Raphael, accelerate my vision, so I can see the aggressive spirit that is attacking me right now, and see how it is forcing me into a reactionary pattern that drains my energy and attention.

> Raphael Archangel, your light so intense,
> raise me beyond all human pretense.
> Mother Mary and you have a vision so bold,
> to see that our highest potential unfold.

**Raphael Archangel, for vision I pray,
Raphael Archangel, show me the way,
Raphael Archangel, your emerald ray,
Raphael Archangel, my life a new day.**

2. Archangel Raphael, accelerate my vision, so I can see the spirit that I have personally created, and how it makes me vulnerable to the collective spirit that is attacking me.

> Raphael Archangel, in emerald sphere,
> to immaculate vision I always adhere.
> Mother Mary enfolds me in her sacred heart,
> from Mother's true love, I am never apart.

**Raphael Archangel, for vision I pray,
Raphael Archangel, show me the way,
Raphael Archangel, your emerald ray,
Raphael Archangel, my life a new day.**

3. Archangel Raphael, accelerate my vision, so I can see the eternal truth, that the pure awareness of the Conscious You can never feel opposed by anything in this world. Thus, whenever I feel opposed, it is actually a spirit within me that feels opposed.

> Raphael Archangel, all ailments you heal,
> each cell in my body in light now you seal.
> Mother Mary's immaculate concept I see,
> perfection of health is real now for me.

**Raphael Archangel, for vision I pray,
Raphael Archangel, show me the way,
Raphael Archangel, your emerald ray,
Raphael Archangel, my life a new day.**

4. Archangel Raphael, accelerate my vision, so I can see the spirit I have created. For I am willing to confront that spirit and slay it, as Saint George slew the dragon.

> Raphael Archangel, your light is so real,
> the vision of Christ in me you reveal.
> Mother Mary now helps me to truly transcend,
> in emerald light with you I ascend.

> **Raphael Archangel, for vision I pray,**
> **Raphael Archangel, show me the way,**
> **Raphael Archangel, your emerald ray,**
> **Raphael Archangel, my life a new day.**

5. Archangel Raphael, accelerate my vision, so I can see the spirit that feels threatened, thus having a need to project into the minds of other people, causing me to seek to change them instead of changing myself.

> With angels I soar,
> as I reach for MORE.
> The angels so real,
> their love all will heal.
> The angels bring peace,
> all conflicts will cease.
> With angels of light,
> we soar to new height.

> **The rustling sound of angel wings,**
> **what joy as even matter sings,**
> **what joy as every atom rings,**
> **in harmony with angel wings.**

6th Ray

1. Archangel Uriel, bind and consume all anti-peace energies in my being, so that I can see how they are projections from aggressive spirits that are aimed at controlling my mind.

> Uriel Archangel, immense is the power,
> of angels of peace, all war to devour.
> The demons of war, no match for your light,
> consuming them all, with radiance so bright.

> **Uriel Archangel, use your great sword,**
> **Uriel Archangel, consume all discord,**
> **Uriel Archangel, we're of one accord,**
> **Uriel Archangel, we walk with the Lord.**

2. Archangel Uriel, shatter the veil of anti-peace, so I can see the aggressive spirit within my own being, the spirit who is directing a force of anti-peace in order to control my mind and the minds of other people.

> Uriel Archangel, intense is the sound,
> when millions of angels, their voices compound.
> They build a crescendo, piercing the night,
> life's glorious oneness revealed to our sight.

> **Uriel Archangel, use your great sword,**
> **Uriel Archangel, consume all discord,**
> **Uriel Archangel, we're of one accord,**
> **Uriel Archangel, we walk with the Lord.**

| *Part Two - Invocations*

3. Archangel Uriel, shatter the veil of anti-peace, so I can see the spirit that is seeking to justify itself through the epic mindset, which makes me believe my attempt to control others is justified by some greater cause.

> Uriel Archangel, from out the Great Throne,
> your millions of trumpets, sound the One Tone.
> Consuming all discord with your harmony,
> the sound of all sounds will set all life free.
>
> **Uriel Archangel, use your great sword,**
> **Uriel Archangel, consume all discord,**
> **Uriel Archangel, we're of one accord,**
> **Uriel Archangel, we walk with the Lord.**

4. Archangel Uriel, bind the spirit that causes me to focus my attention on changing something outside myself, and seeking to justify this by the dualistic logic and the relative value judgments of the serpentine mind.

> Uriel Archangel, all war is now gone,
> for you bring a message, from heart of the One
> The hearts of all men, now singing in peace,
> the spirals of love, forever increase.
>
> **Uriel Archangel, use your great sword,**
> **Uriel Archangel, consume all discord,**
> **Uriel Archangel, we're of one accord,**
> **Uriel Archangel, we walk with the Lord.**

5. Archangel Uriel, I will from now on focus all attention on changing my own state of consciousness, slaying the spirits I have created and embodying the positive lessons of the seven rays. Help me find the inner peace to focus on changing myself.

> With angels I soar,
> as I reach for MORE.
> The angels so real,
> their love all will heal.
> The angels bring peace,
> all conflicts will cease.
> With angels of light,
> we soar to new height.
>
> **The rustling sound of angel wings,**
> **what joy as even matter sings,**
> **what joy as every atom rings,**
> **in harmony with angel wings.**

7th Ray

1. Archangel Zadkiel, shatter the veil of anti-freedom, so I can experience the full truth, that I will never be free until I have confronted and slain all of the spirits that lurk in my subconscious mind.

> Zadkiel Archangel, your flow is so swift,
> in your violet light, I instantly shift,
> into a vibration in which I am free,
> from all limitations of the lesser me.
>
> **Zadkiel Archangel, encircle the earth,**
> **Zadkiel Archangel, with your violet girth,**
> **Zadkiel Archangel, unstoppable mirth,**
> **Zadkiel Archangel, our planet's rebirth.**

| *Part Two - Invocations*

2. Archangel Zadkiel, accelerate me beyond all fear, guilt and shame and help me accept that creating these spirits is an inevitable part of taking embodiment on a dense planet like earth.

> Zadkiel Archangel, I truly aspire,
> to being the master of your violet fire.
> Wielding the power, of your alchemy,
> I use Sacred Word, to set all life free.
>
> **Zadkiel Archangel, encircle the earth,**
> **Zadkiel Archangel, with your violet girth,**
> **Zadkiel Archangel, unstoppable mirth,**
> **Zadkiel Archangel, our planet's rebirth.**

3. Archangel Zadkiel, I refuse to feed my energies and attention into the spirits in my being. Accelerate my inner knowing that by letting these spirits die, I will not die but will be reborn into the total freedom of pure, innocent awareness.

> Zadkiel Archangel, your violet light,
> transforming the earth, with unstoppable might.
> So swiftly our planet, beginning to spin,
> with legions of angels, our victory we win.
>
> **Zadkiel Archangel, encircle the earth,**
> **Zadkiel Archangel, with your violet girth,**
> **Zadkiel Archangel, unstoppable mirth,**
> **Zadkiel Archangel, our planet's rebirth.**

4. Archangel Zadkiel, accelerate me into the freedom of knowing that I only need to deal with one false spirit right now, and when I always seek to transcend my current spirit, I will remain on the true path back to Oneness.

> Zadkiel Archangel, your violet flame,
> the earth and humanity, never the same.
> Saint Germain's Golden Age, is a reality,
> what glorious wonder, I joyously see.
>
> **Zadkiel Archangel, encircle the earth,**
> **Zadkiel Archangel, with your violet girth,**
> **Zadkiel Archangel, unstoppable mirth,**
> **Zadkiel Archangel, our planet's rebirth.**

5. Archangel Zadkiel, accelerate my entire consciousness, being and world, so that I effortlessly leave behind false spirits and rise into the complete innocence with which I first descended into the material world. For I am willing to be accelerated into Oneness.

> With angels I soar,
> as I reach for MORE.
> The angels so real,
> their love all will heal.
> The angels bring peace,
> all conflicts will cease.
> With angels of light,
> we soar to new height.
>
> **The rustling sound of angel wings,**
> **what joy as even matter sings,**
> **what joy as every atom rings,**
> **in harmony with angel wings.**

Oneness Decree

In the name I AM THAT I AM, Jesus Christ, I acknowledge that the only way to grow to the next level of my path, is that I must deal with the negative, aggressive spirit that corresponds to my current level. In order to free myself from the downward pull of that spirit, I must look at the spirit of my outer self, and see it as a spirit that is different from the Conscious You, different from the real me. I thus consciously and deliberately say to that spirit: "I am not you, and I do not want to see life through the filter that you are. I acknowledge that you are unreal, and I am willing to let you die, so that I can be free to rise to a higher level." To this end, I decree:

1. Surya, thou perfectly balanced one,
shining your light like a radiant sun,
from the God Star infusing the Earth
with unstoppable power, producing rebirth.

**Oh Alpha-Omega in Great Central Sun,
release now the Infinite Power of One,
to shatter the veil of duality's lies,
cutting all people free from its ties.**

**Beloved Surya, your balancing power,
flooding the Earth like a radiant shower,
as Father and Mother in oneness we see,
in infinite bliss forever we'll be.**

2. Resurrecting the feminine in woman and man,
revealing the matrix of God's perfect plan,
consuming all images graven and old,
raising religion beyond earthly mold.

**Oh Alpha-Omega in Great Central Sun,
release now the Infinite Power of One,
to shatter the veil of duality's lies,
cutting all people free from its ties.**

**Beloved Surya, your balancing power,
flooding the Earth like a radiant shower,
as Father and Mother in oneness we see,
in infinite bliss forever we'll be.**

3. Saint Germain's Golden Age a reality at last,
the lies of duality a thing of the past,
the Mother Divine is raised up in all,
who listen within and follow the call.

**Oh Alpha-Omega in Great Central Sun,
release now the Infinite Power of One,
to shatter the veil of duality's lies,
cutting all people free from its ties.**

**Beloved Surya, your balancing power,
flooding the Earth like a radiant shower,
as Father and Mother in oneness we see,
in infinite bliss forever we'll be.**

4. Maraytaii is the name of the Mother Divine,
who calls all her children to let their light shine,
with Jesus we now take the ultimate stand,
affirming the Kingdom of God is at hand.

**Oh Alpha-Omega in Great Central Sun,
release now the Infinite Power of One,
to shatter the veil of duality's lies,
cutting all people free from its ties.**

**Beloved Surya, your balancing power,
flooding the Earth like a radiant shower,
as Father and Mother in oneness we see,
in infinite bliss forever we'll be.**

5. Mother Mary is showing all people the way,
to the kingdom within through the feminine ray,
for when we see God within every form,
we know that abundance is truly the norm.

| *Part Two - Invocations*

> Oh Alpha-Omega in Great Central Sun,
> release now the Infinite Power of One,
> to shatter the veil of duality's lies,
> cutting all people free from its ties.
>
> Beloved Surya, your balancing power,
> flooding the Earth like a radiant shower,
> as Father and Mother in oneness we see,
> in infinite bliss forever we'll be.

6. And now we are led by the great Master MORE,
across the vast sea to a welcoming shore,
where all of duality's voices will cease,
as with the Lord Buddha we're centered in peace.

> Oh Alpha-Omega in Great Central Sun,
> release now the Infinite Power of One,
> to shatter the veil of duality's lies,
> cutting all people free from its ties.
>
> Beloved Surya, your balancing power,
> flooding the Earth like a radiant shower,
> as Father and Mother in oneness we see,
> in infinite bliss forever we'll be.

7. As Alpha-Omega their union reveal,
we know separation cannot be real,
and thus we can enter the Great Central Sun,
where ultimate victory of union is won.

> Oh Alpha-Omega in Great Central Sun,
> release now the Infinite Power of One,
> to shatter the veil of duality's lies,
> cutting all people free from its ties.
>
> Beloved Surya, your balancing power,
> flooding the Earth like a radiant shower,
> as Father and Mother in oneness we see,
> in infinite bliss forever we'll be.

8. And thus we go forth to proclaim the great plan,
to bridge separation between God and Man.
Accepting the call co-creators to be,
as we raise the Earth to her God-victory.

**Oh Alpha-Omega in Great Central Sun,
release now the Infinite Power of One,
to shatter the veil of duality's lies,
cutting all people free from its ties.**

**Beloved Surya, your balancing power,
flooding the Earth like a radiant shower,
as Father and Mother in oneness we see,
in infinite bliss forever we'll be.**

Sealing:

In the name of the Divine Mother, I call to the seven Archangels for the protection and sealing of myself and all people in my circle of influence from any backlash from the forces judged by this invocation. I call for the multiplication of my calls by the entire Spirit of the Ascended Masters, so that we form the perfect figure-eight flow of "As Above, so below." Thus, I accept that this is fully manifest, because the mouth of the Lord, the Christ within me, has spoken it. Amen.

INVOCATION FOR LETTING GO OF SPIRITS

In the name I AM THAT I AM, Jesus Christ, I call to my I AM Presence to flow through the I Will Be Presence that I AM and give this invocation with full power. I call to the seven Elohim to release the creative energies of the seven rays and consume in my being all spirits that are perversions of the rays, including all thought matrices that block my creative powers:

[Make personal calls]

God is Father and Mother
God is Father, God is Mother,
never one without the other.

Your balanced union is our source,
your Love will keep us on our course.
You offer us abundant life,
to free us from all sense of strife.
We plunge ourselves into the stream,
awakening from this bad dream.
We see that life is truly one,
and thus our victory is won.
We have returned unto our God,
on the path the saints have trod.
We form God's body on the Earth,
and give our planet its rebirth,
into a Golden Age of Love,
with ample blessings from Above.
We set all people free to see
that oneness is reality,
and in that oneness we will be
whole for all eternity.
And now the Earth is truly healed,
all life in God's perfection sealed.

God is Father, God is Mother,
we see God in each other.

1st Ray

1. God is a Spirit, and I am willing to know my Creator in Spirit and in Truth.

> 1. O Hercules Blue, you fill every space,
> with infinite Power and infinite Grace,
> you embody the key to creativity,
> the will to transcend into Infinity.
>
> **O Hercules Blue, in oneness with thee,**
> **I open my heart to your reality,**
> **in feeling your flame, so clearly I see,**
> **transcending my self is the true alchemy.**

2. I am a self-aware Spirit, and have complete free will to transcend myself at any moment, moving ever closer to oneness with my Creator.

> 2. O Hercules Blue, I lovingly raise,
> my voice in giving God infinite praise,
> I'm grateful for playing my personal part,
> In God's infinitely intricate work of art.
>
> **O Hercules Blue, all life now you heal,**
> **enveloping all in your Blue-flame Seal,**
> **your electric-blue fire within us reveal,**
> **our innermost longing for all that is real.**

3. I am a co-creative Spirit, and I co-create by creating a spirit at my current level of consciousness.

> 3. O Hercules Blue, I pledge now my life,
> in helping this planet transcend human strife,
> duality's lies are pierced by your light,
> restoring the fullness of my inner sight.
>
> **O Hercules Blue, I'm one with your will,**
> **all space in my being with Blue Flame you fill,**
> **your power allows me to forge on until,**
> **I pierce every veil and climb every hill.**

4. The spirit I create does not have self-awareness, so although it can evolve, it cannot transcend the thought matrix that defines it.

> 4. O Hercules Blue, your Temple of Light,
> revealed to us all through our inner sight,
> a beacon that radiates light to the Earth,
> bringing about our planet's rebirth.
>
> **O Hercules Blue, all life you defend,**
> **giving us power to always transcend,**
> **in you the expansion of self has no end,**
> **as I in God's infinite spirals ascend.**

5. I have self-awareness, and thus I see that the only way for me to rise to a higher level of consciousness, is to let go of the spirit I created at my current level. If I do not let that spirit die, my attention and creative energies will be consumed in growing that spirit.

> **Accelerate into Creativity, I AM real,**
> **Accelerate into Creativity, all life heal,**
> **Accelerate into Creativity, I AM MORE,**
> **Accelerate into Creativity, all will soar.**

Accelerate into Creativity! (3X)
Beloved Hercules and Amazonia.

Accelerate into Creativity! (3X)
Beloved Michael and Faith.

Accelerate into Creativity! (3X)
Beloved Master MORE.

Accelerate into Creativity! (3X)
Beloved I AM.

2nd Ray

1. I recognize that any spirit has a certain survival instinct, and thus it will seek to keep me attached to or blinded by the thought matrix that defines the spirit.

> 1. Beloved Apollo, with your second ray,
> you open my eyes to see a new day,
> I see through duality's lies and deceit,
> transcending the mindset producing defeat.
>
> **Beloved Apollo, thou Elohim Gold,**
> **your radiant light my eyes now behold,**
> **as pages of wisdom you gently unfold,**
> **I feel I am free from all that is old.**

2. The spirit will project at me, that I will die if the spirit dies. Yet I know I am a self-aware Spirit, and thus I am more than my own creation. Thus, I will not die by letting a spirit die; I will be free to be MORE.

> 2. Beloved Apollo, in your flame I know,
> that your living wisdom is always a flow,
> in your light I see my own highest will,
> immersed in the stream that never stands still.

| *Part Two - Invocations*

> Beloved Apollo, your light makes it clear,
> why we have taken embodiment here,
> working to raise our own cosmic sphere,
> together we form the tip of the spear.

3. I am indeed willing to let the spirit I have created die, so I can be reborn into a higher sense of self.

> 3. Beloved Apollo, exposing all lies,
> I hereby surrender all ego-based ties,
> I know my perception is truly the key,
> to transcending the serpentine duality.

> Beloved Apollo, we heed now your call,
> drawing us into Wisdom's Great Hall,
> exposing all lies causing the fall,
> you help us reclaim the oneness of all.

4. I take full responsibility for the fact, that I have created that spirit, and that I am hanging on the cross of the thought matrix that defines the spirit, and thus sets boundaries for my creative expression.

> 4. Beloved Apollo, your wisdom so clear,
> in oneness with you, no serpent I fear,
> the beam in my eye I'm willing to see,
> I'm free from the serpent's own duality.

> Beloved Apollo, my eyes now I raise,
> I see that the Earth is in a new phase,
> I willingly stand in your piercing gaze,
> empowered, I exit duality's maze.

5. I accept that no one is going to take me down from that cross, and thus I give up the ghost of my current spirit.

Accelerate my Awakeness, I AM real,
Accelerate my Awakeness, all life heal,
Accelerate my Awakeness, I AM MORE,
Accelerate my Awakeness, all will soar.

Accelerate my Awakeness! (3X)
Beloved Apollo and Lumina.

Accelerate my Awakeness! (3X)
Beloved Jophiel and Christine.

Accelerate my Awakeness! (3X)
Beloved Master Lanto.

Accelerate my Awakeness! (3X)
Beloved I AM.

3rd Ray

1. I am a co-creative Spirit, and thus I have a love for creating something that is more than what I have created before.

1. O Heros-Amora, in your love so pink,
I care not what others about me may think,
in oneness with you, I claim a new day,
an innocent child, I frolic and play.

O Heros-Amora, a new life begun,
I laugh at the devil, the serious one,
I bathe in your glorious Ruby-Pink Sun,
knowing my God allows life to be fun.

2. I know the only way to create more is to let go of the spirit, that limits my creative expression to a certain matrix.

> 2. O Heros-Amora, life is such a joy,
> I see that the world is like a great toy,
> whatever my mind into it projects,
> the mirror of life exactly reflects.
>
> **O Heros-Amora, I reap what I sow,**
> **yet this is Plan B for helping me grow,**
> **for truly, Plan A is that I join the flow,**
> **immersed in the Infinite Love you bestow.**

3. I love oneness with my Creator more than anything I have created in this world. And thus, I can lovingly leave my creation behind and let the spirit die.

> 3. O Heros-Amora, conditions you burn,
> I know I AM free to take a new turn,
> Immersed in the stream of infinite Love,
> I know that my Spirit came from Above.
>
> **O Heros-Amora, awakened I see,**
> **in true love is no conditionality,**
> **the devil is stuck in his duality,**
> **but I AM set free by Love's reality.**

4. I am detaching myself from the spirit I have created, knowing that it is just a vehicle, knowing it is a servant that I have created, and that I – the Conscious You – am in charge.

> 4. O Heros-Amora, I feel that at last,
> I've risen above the trap of my past,
> in true love I claim my freedom to grow,
> forever I'm one with Love's Infinite Flow.

O Heros-Amora, conditions are ties,
forming a net of serpentine lies,
your love has no bounds, forever it flies,
raising all life into Ruby-Pink skies.

5. I know I am not the spirit I have created, and thus I will no longer magnify or reinforce that spirit. I will indeed let it die out of pure love, without feeling this is in any way forced upon me.

Accelerate into Oneness, I AM real,
Accelerate into Oneness, all life heal,
Accelerate into Oneness, I AM MORE,
Accelerate into Oneness, all will soar.

Accelerate into Oneness! (3X)
Beloved Heros and Amora.

Accelerate into Oneness! (3X)
Beloved Chamuel and Charity.

Accelerate into Oneness! (3X)
Beloved Paul the Venetian.

Accelerate into Oneness! (3X)
Beloved I AM.

4th Ray

1. I am accelerating my love, so that I am willing to lay down my current spirit in order to raise the whole.

1. Beloved Astrea, your heart is so true,
your Circle and Sword of white and blue,
cut all life free from dramas unwise,
on wings of Purity our planet will rise.

| *Part Two - Invocations*

> **Beloved Astrea, in God Purity,**
> **accelerate all of my life energy,**
> **raising my mind into true unity**
> **with the Masters of love in Infinity.**

2. I hereby shine the light of my I AM Presence, the light of the seven rays, into the caves of the subconscious mind, flushing out the spirits into the open, so that I can see them.

> 2. Beloved Astrea, from Purity's Ray,
> send forth deliverance to all life today,
> acceleration to Purity, I AM now free
> from all that is less than love's Purity.
>
> **Beloved Astrea, in oneness with you,**
> **your circle and sword of electric blue,**
> **with Purity's Light cutting right through,**
> **raising within me all that is true.**

3. I am willing to see any spirit that causes me to direct my attention outside myself, seeking to change other people or the world instead of transcending my sense of self.

> 3. Beloved Astrea, accelerate us all,
> as for your deliverance I fervently call,
> set all life free from vision impure
> beyond fear and doubt, I AM rising for sure.
>
> **Beloved Astrea, I AM willing to see,**
> **all of the lies that keep me unfree,**
> **I AM rising beyond every impurity,**
> **with Purity's Light forever in me.**

4. I acknowledge that the pure self that descended is more than my current outer self, which is made up of many individual spirits that do not have self-awareness.

> 4. Beloved Astrea, accelerate life
> beyond all duality's struggle and strife,
> consume all division between God and man,
> accelerate fulfillment of God's perfect plan.
>
> **Beloved Astrea, I lovingly call,**
> **break down separation's invisible wall,**
> **I surrender all lies causing the fall,**
> **forever affirming the oneness of All.**

5. I am indeed willing to let my I AM Presence and the ascended masters, lead me on the path of gradually letting these spirits die, so I return to my pure identity as being an open door for my I AM Presence.

> **Accelerate into Purity, I AM real,**
> **Accelerate into Purity, all life heal,**
> **Accelerate into Purity, I AM MORE,**
> **Accelerate into Purity, all will soar.**
>
> **Accelerate into Purity! (3X)**
> Beloved Elohim Astrea.
>
> **Accelerate into Purity! (3X)**
> Beloved Gabriel and Hope.
>
> **Accelerate into Purity! (3X)**
> Beloved Serapis Bey.
>
> **Accelerate into Purity! (3X)**
> Beloved I AM.

| *Part Two - Invocations*

5th Ray

1. I am from now on engaged in the true path of coming to see the limiting spirits, and then detaching myself from all identification with them.

> 1. Cyclopea so dear, the truth you reveal,
> the truth that duality's ailments will heal,
> your Emerald Light is like a great balm,
> my emotional body is perfectly calm.
>
> **Cyclopea so dear, in Emerald Sphere,**
> **to vision so clear I always adhere,**
> **in raising perception I shall persevere,**
> **as deep in my heart your truth I revere.**

2. I will no longer participate in the impossible quest, of seeking to get the world or other people to conform to the perception filter of my current outer self. Instead, I will surrender the matrices behind that perception filter.

> 2. Cyclopea so dear, with you I unwind,
> all negative spirals clouding my mind,
> I know pure awareness is truly my core,
> the key to becoming the wide-open door.
>
> **Cyclopea so dear, clear my inner sight,**
> **empowered, I pierce the soul's fearful night,**
> **through veils of duality I now take flight,**
> **bathed in your penetrating Emerald Light.**

3. I consciously give up the illusion of my ego, that if the world acknowledges the perfection of a spirit, then God must let that spirit into heaven.

> 3. Cyclopea so dear, life can only reflect,
> the images that my mind does project,
> the key to my healing is clearing the mind,
> from the images my ego is hiding behind.
>
> **Cyclopea so dear, I want to aim high,**
> **to your healing flame I ever draw nigh,**
> **I now see my life through your single eye,**
> **beyond all disease I AM ready to fly.**

4. I acknowledge that no separate spirit can ever enter heaven. I acknowledge that neither my ego nor any spirit can fool God.

> 4. Cyclopea so dear, your Emerald Flame,
> exposes every subtle, dualistic power game,
> including the game of wanting to say,
> that truth is defined in only one way.
>
> **Cyclopea so dear, I am feeling the flow,**
> **as your Living Truth upon me you bestow,**
> **I know truth transcends all systems below,**
> **immersed in your light, I continue to grow.**

5. I acknowledge that any separate spirit is defined by conditions, and that these conditions cannot be brought into heaven. Thus, I surrender all of my conditions, for I long to return to the unconditional innocence that I AM.

> **Accelerate into Wholeness, I AM real,**
> **Accelerate into Wholeness, all life heal,**
> **Accelerate into Wholeness, I AM MORE,**
> **Accelerate into Wholeness, all will soar.**

Accelerate into Wholeness! (3X)
Beloved Cyclopea and Virginia.

Accelerate into Wholeness! (3X)
Beloved Raphael and Mary.

Accelerate into Wholeness! (3X)
Beloved Master Hilarion.

Accelerate into Wholeness! (3X)
Beloved I AM.

6th Ray

1. I know that a separate spirit is by definition mortal, but it dreams of immortality. It dreams of living up to some condition, whereby it becomes acceptable to God and therefore gains entry into the wedding feast with Christ.

> 1. O Elohim Peace, in Unity's Flame,
> there is no more room for duality's game,
> we know that all form is from the same source,
> empowering us to plot a new course.
>
> **O Elohim Peace, the bell now you ring,**
> **causing all atoms to vibrate and sing,**
> **I now see that there is no separate thing,**
> **to my ego-based self I no longer cling.**

2. I know that the ultimate dream of the ego, of the fallen beings, and of the separate spirits is that they can somehow be perfected in the eyes of God.

> 2. O Elohim Peace, you help me to know,
> that Jesus has come your Flame to bestow,
> upon all who are ready to give up the strife,
> by following Christ into infinite life.

> O Elohim Peace, through your eyes I see,
> that only in oneness will I ever be free,
> I give up the sense of a separate me,
> I AM crossing Samsara's turbulent sea.

3. I know that any separate spirit is based on a static, conditional definition of perfection. Yet God's concept of perfection is the ongoing self-transcendence of the River of Life, which is constantly seeking to transcend any condition that keeps it from Oneness.

> 3. O Elohim Peace, you show me the way,
> for clearing my mind from duality's fray,
> you pierce the illusions of both time and space,
> separation consumed by your Infinite Grace.
>
> O Elohim Peace, what beauty your name,
> consuming within me duality's shame,
> It was through the vibration of your Golden Flame,
> that Christ the illusion of death overcame.

4. I acknowledge that only a separate spirit can feel the fear of death, whereas the real me, the pure awareness of the Conscious You, cannot fear death because it knows it is out of the Creator's Being.

> 4. O Elohim Peace, you bring now to Earth,
> the unstoppable flame of Cosmic Rebirth,
> I give up the sense that something is mine,
> allowing your Light through my being to shine.
>
> O Elohim Peace, through your tranquility,
> we are free from the chaos of duality,
> in oneness with God a new identity,
> we are raising the Earth into Infinity.

5. I hereby give up the entire quest for conditional perfection, and the desire to prove any spirit right by proving any other spirit wrong.

> Accelerate into Unity, I AM real,
> Accelerate into Unity, all life heal,
> Accelerate into Unity, I AM MORE,
> Accelerate into Unity, all will soar.
>
> **Accelerate into Unity! (3X)**
> Beloved Peace and Aloha.
>
> **Accelerate into Unity! (3X)**
> Beloved Uriel and Aurora.
>
> **Accelerate into Unity! (3X)**
> Beloved Jesus and Nada.
>
> **Accelerate into Unity! (3X)**
> Beloved I AM.

7th Ray

1. I see that what takes away my creative freedom is the quest of these separate spirits to validate themselves.

> 1. Beloved Arcturus, release now the flow,
> of Violet Flame to help all life grow,
> in ever-expanding circles of Light,
> it pulses within every atom so bright.
>
> **Beloved Arcturus, thou Elohim Free,**
> **I open my heart to your reality,**
> **expanding my heart into Infinity,**
> **your flame is the key to my God-victory.**

2. I see that a separate spirit is seeking to validate itself by using the conditional matrix that defined it. The spirit and the ego see the world through this matrix, so they believe they are always right. Yet God will never agree, and thus the quest is futile.

> 2. Beloved Arcturus, be with me alway,
> reborn, I am ready to face a new day,
> I have no attachments to life here on Earth,
> I claim a new life in your Flame of Rebirth.
>
> **Beloved Arcturus, your Violet Flame pure,**
> **is for every ailment the ultimate cure,**
> **against it no darkness could ever endure,**
> **my freedom it will forever ensure.**

3. I have had enough of trying to prove myself right in the conditional world of separate spirits. I want to prove myself right in the real world of constant self-transcendence.

> 3. Beloved Arcturus, your bright violet fire,
> now fills every atom, raising them higher,
> the space in each atom all filled with your light,
> as matter itself is shining so bright.
>
> **Beloved Arcturus, your transforming Grace,**
> **empowers me now every challenge to face,**
> **as your violet light floods my inner space,**
> **towards my ascension I willingly race.**

4. I hereby surrender the very standard that causes me to move towards the separate spirits I have created, the spirits that lie in wait to try to entrap me, like the sirens with their beguiling song. For I will no longer be shipwrecked on the cliffs.

> 4. Beloved Arcturus, bring in a new age,
> help Earth and humanity turn a new page,
> your transforming light gives me certainty,
> Saint Germain's Golden Age is a reality.
>
> **Beloved Arcturus, I surrender all fear,**
> **I AM feeling your Presence so tangibly near,**
> **with your Freedom's Song filling my ear,**
> **I know that to God I AM ever so dear.**

5. I hereby consciously choose to no longer identify myself with the false path of seeking to perfect any given spirit. Instead, I fully engage myself in the path of ongoing self-transcendence, as I flow joyfully and effortlessly with the River of Life.

> **Accelerate into Freedom, I AM real,**
> **Accelerate into Freedom, all life heal,**
> **Accelerate into Freedom, I AM MORE,**
> **Accelerate into Freedom, all will soar.**
>
> **Accelerate into Freedom! (3X)**
> Beloved Arcturus and Victoria.
>
> **Accelerate into Freedom! (3X)**
> Beloved Zadkiel and Amethyst.
>
> **Accelerate into Freedom! (3X)**
> Beloved Saint Germain.
>
> **Accelerate into Freedom! (3X)**
> Beloved I AM.

I AM being More

River of Life, abundant flow
with your light I am aglow.
I am flowing—I am growing,
one with your eternal knowing.

Fill my space—with your grace,
I am in my rightful place.
I will BE—forever free,
my God plan I always see.

Sacred dove—from above,
no conditions in God's love.
As I call—light does fall,
raising up the Christ in all.

Life is sealed—all are healed,
God's perfection is revealed.
We begin—without sin,
one with God, we will win.

Life is one—God has won,
a new day has begun.
Sacred light—oh so bright,
everything is now set right.

Earth is free—now to BE,
Freedom's Star for all to see.
Always MORE—than before,
River of Life I do adore.

I AM MORE—forevermore,
the Flow of Life I do restore.
River of life, through the Son,
Father, Mother are as one.

(Give 1 time, 3 times or more.)

| *Part Two - Invocations*

Sealing:

In the name of the seven Elohim, I am the open door for the creative flow of all seven rays, expressing themselves through my being in a completely balanced manifestation. In balance I am, and in balance I remain, this day and forevermore—as I become MORE without ever seeking to hold on to anything in this world. Thus, in constant self-transcendence, I am sealed in the creative flow of the River of Life. Amen.

Invocation for Exposing Spirits in my Being

In the name I AM THAT I AM, Jesus Christ, I call to my I AM Presence to flow through the I Will Be Presence that I AM and give this invocation with full power. I call to the beloved Maha Chohan to help me see and dis-identify myself from the spirit that is currently holding back my spiritual progress, including…

[Make personal calls]

God is Father and Mother
God is Father, God is Mother,
never one without the other.

Your balanced union is our source,
your Love will keep us on our course.
You offer us abundant life,
to free us from all sense of strife.
We plunge ourselves into the stream,
awakening from this bad dream.
We see that life is truly one,
and thus our victory is won.
We have returned unto our God,
on the path the saints have trod.
We form God's body on the Earth,
and give our planet its rebirth,
into a Golden Age of Love,
with ample blessings from Above.
We set all people free to see
that oneness is reality,
and in that oneness we will be
whole for all eternity.
And now the Earth is truly healed,
all life in God's perfection sealed.

Part Two - Invocations

God is Father, God is Mother,
we see God in each other.

Part 1

1. Maha Chohan, I accept that I am a co-creator with my God and that I am designed to co-create.

Maha Chohan, I will to grow,
I feel the power of your flow.
Maha Chohan, the veil is rent,
creative will from heaven sent.

**O Holy Spirit, flow through me,
I am the open door for thee.
O mighty rushing stream of Light,
transcendence is my sacred right.**

2. Maha Chohan, I accept that I can co-create because I have self-awareness, and thus I can formulate mental images.

Maha Chohan, your wisdom streams,
awaken all from matter's dreams.
Maha Chohan, your balance bring,
let bells of integration ring.

**O Holy Spirit, flow through me,
I am the open door for thee.
O mighty rushing stream of Light,
transcendence is my sacred right.**

3. Maha Chohan, I see that my co-creation is limited by my imagination, and I want to free my imagination, so I can envision images from the Christ mind.

> Maha Chohan, love's mighty call,
> the prison walls are shattered all.
> Maha Chohan, set all life free
> through unconditionality.
>
> **O Holy Spirit, flow through me,**
> **I am the open door for thee.**
> **O mighty rushing stream of Light,**
> **transcendence is my sacred right.**

4. Maha Chohan, I declare that I am willing to free my subconscious mind from all that limits my imagination, and keeps it trapped in the mind of anti-christ.

> Maha Chohan, intentions pure,
> all life is one, I know for sure.
> Maha Chohan, I am awake,
> surrender all for oneness' sake.
>
> **O Holy Spirit, flow through me,**
> **I am the open door for thee.**
> **O mighty rushing stream of Light,**
> **transcendence is my sacred right.**

5. Maha Chohan, I understand that I co-create, by projecting a mental image upon the Ma-ter light.

> Maha Chohan, help all men see,
> through veils of unreality.
> Maha Chohan, with single eye,
> I know I am the greater "I."

> O Holy Spirit, flow through me,
> I am the open door for thee.
> O mighty rushing stream of Light,
> transcendence is my sacred right.

6. Maha Chohan, I understand that I constantly have mental images in the four levels of my mind, and thus I am constantly co-creating.

> Maha Chohan, your peace I find,
> Maitreya shows me to be kind.
> Maha Chohan, all war will cease,
> now flooding all with sacred peace.

> O Holy Spirit, flow through me,
> I am the open door for thee.
> O mighty rushing stream of Light,
> transcendence is my sacred right.

7. Maha Chohan, I declare that I am willing to become more conscious of the fact that I co-create by creating spirits.

> Maha Chohan, you balance all,
> the seven rays upon my call.
> Maha Chohan, all life is free,
> transcending for eternity.

> O Holy Spirit, flow through me,
> I am the open door for thee.
> O mighty rushing stream of Light,
> transcendence is my sacred right.

8. Maha Chohan, I understand that I have created many spirits in the identity, mental and emotional levels of my mind. I want to be free from these spirits and be the open door for my I AM Presence.

> Maha Chohan, your sacred Flame,
> what beauty in your blessed name.
> Maha Chohan, what rushing flow,
> the Spirit one with life below.

> **O Holy Spirit, flow through me,**
> **I am the open door for thee.**
> **O mighty rushing stream of Light,**
> **transcendence is my sacred right.**

Part 2

1. Maha Chohan, I understand that the light and consciousness from my I AM Presence will stream through the spirits in my subconscious mind, which will make those spirits stronger and stronger.

> Maha Chohan, I will to grow,
> I feel the power of your flow.
> Maha Chohan, the veil is rent,
> creative will from heaven sent.

> **O Holy Spirit, flow through me,**
> **I am the open door for thee.**
> **O mighty rushing stream of Light,**
> **transcendence is my sacred right.**

| *Part Two - Invocations*

2. Maha Chohan, I am willing to walk the spiritual path in a more conscious manner, and gradually dis-identify myself from the spirits I have created.

> Maha Chohan, your wisdom streams,
> awaken all from matter's dreams.
> Maha Chohan, your balance bring,
> let bells of integration ring.
>
> **O Holy Spirit, flow through me,**
> **I am the open door for thee.**
> **O mighty rushing stream of Light,**
> **transcendence is my sacred right.**

3. Maha Chohan, I understand that as long as I am identified with a given spirit, my consciousness will stream through it, which means that I cannot see that spirit from the outside.

> Maha Chohan, love's mighty call,
> the prison walls are shattered all.
> Maha Chohan, set all life free
> through unconditionality.
>
> **O Holy Spirit, flow through me,**
> **I am the open door for thee.**
> **O mighty rushing stream of Light,**
> **transcendence is my sacred right.**

4. Maha Chohan, I understand that when I do not see a spirit, and do not see it as separate from myself, I cannot free myself from it.

> Maha Chohan, intentions pure,
> all life is one, I know for sure.
> Maha Chohan, I am awake,
> surrender all for oneness' sake.

**O Holy Spirit, flow through me,
I am the open door for thee.
O mighty rushing stream of Light,
transcendence is my sacred right.**

5. Maha Chohan, I understand that when my consciousness streams through a spirit, my energies are tied up in the spirit, and it becomes more difficult for me to pull myself outside the spirit and see it for what it is.

Maha Chohan, help all men see,
through veils of unreality.
Maha Chohan, with single eye,
I know I am the greater "I."

**O Holy Spirit, flow through me,
I am the open door for thee.
O mighty rushing stream of Light,
transcendence is my sacred right.**

6. Maha Chohan, help me make use of my ability to project myself outside the spirit with which I am currently identified.

Maha Chohan, your peace I find,
Maitreya shows me to be kind.
Maha Chohan, all war will cease,
now flooding all with sacred peace.

**O Holy Spirit, flow through me,
I am the open door for thee.
O mighty rushing stream of Light,
transcendence is my sacred right.**

| *Part Two - Invocations*

7. Maha Chohan, help me pull myself away from the spirit that is currently limiting my progress, so that my self-awareness is no longer focused through that spirit.

> Maha Chohan, you balance all,
> the seven rays upon my call.
> Maha Chohan, all life is free,
> transcending for eternity.
>
> **O Holy Spirit, flow through me,**
> **I am the open door for thee.**
> **O mighty rushing stream of Light,**
> **transcendence is my sacred right.**

8. Maha Chohan, I hereby consciously make the decision, that I will engage in the process of pulling myself away from identification with this spirit, so that I can come to see it from the outside.

> Maha Chohan, your sacred Flame,
> what beauty in your blessed name.
> Maha Chohan, what rushing flow,
> the Spirit one with life below.
>
> **O Holy Spirit, flow through me,**
> **I am the open door for thee.**
> **O mighty rushing stream of Light,**
> **transcendence is my sacred right.**

Part 3

1. Maha Chohan, I hereby declare that I do not want to be like this anymore. I do not want to continue to repeat these old patterns. I want to change. I want to be more than this.

> Maha Chohan, I will to grow,
> I feel the power of your flow.
> Maha Chohan, the veil is rent,
> creative will from heaven sent.
>
> **O Holy Spirit, flow through me,**
> **I am the open door for thee.**
> **O mighty rushing stream of Light,**
> **transcendence is my sacred right.**

2. Maha Chohan, I am willing to see something I have never seen before, see that the spirit is not me and thus instantly shift my consciousness, so I no longer identify with the spirit at my present level of the path.

> Maha Chohan, your wisdom streams,
> awaken all from matter's dreams.
> Maha Chohan, your balance bring,
> let bells of integration ring.
>
> **O Holy Spirit, flow through me,**
> **I am the open door for thee.**
> **O mighty rushing stream of Light,**
> **transcendence is my sacred right.**

| *Part Two - Invocations*

3. Maha Chohan, I am indeed willing to rise to the next level towards the 144th level of consciousness, by dis-identifying myself from the spirit at my current level.

> Maha Chohan, love's mighty call,
> the prison walls are shattered all.
> Maha Chohan, set all life free
> through unconditionality.

> **O Holy Spirit, flow through me,**
> **I am the open door for thee.**
> **O mighty rushing stream of Light,**
> **transcendence is my sacred right.**

4. Maha Chohan, I am no longer willing to use my spiritual efforts to reinforce the spirit at my current level of consciousness. I want to come up higher.

> Maha Chohan, intentions pure,
> all life is one, I know for sure.
> Maha Chohan, I am awake,
> surrender all for oneness' sake.

> **O Holy Spirit, flow through me,**
> **I am the open door for thee.**
> **O mighty rushing stream of Light,**
> **transcendence is my sacred right.**

5. Maha Chohan, I am no longer willing to educate the spirit at my current level, so that it supposedly becomes more spiritual. Instead, I want to make true progress by transcending that spirit.

> Maha Chohan, help all men see,
> through veils of unreality.
> Maha Chohan, with single eye,
> I know I am the greater "I."

**O Holy Spirit, flow through me,
I am the open door for thee.
O mighty rushing stream of Light,
transcendence is my sacred right.**

6. Maha Chohan, I no longer want to be on the false path, and thus I am willing to leave behind my current spirit, no matter how spiritual or sophisticated it might seem.

Maha Chohan, your peace I find,
Maitreya shows me to be kind.
Maha Chohan, all war will cease,
now flooding all with sacred peace.

**O Holy Spirit, flow through me,
I am the open door for thee.
O mighty rushing stream of Light,
transcendence is my sacred right.**

7. Maha Chohan, help me dis-identify with this spirit and quickly catch up to my natural level. I am willing to leave behind the spirit and let it die.

Maha Chohan, you balance all,
the seven rays upon my call.
Maha Chohan, all life is free,
transcending for eternity.

**O Holy Spirit, flow through me,
I am the open door for thee.
O mighty rushing stream of Light,
transcendence is my sacred right.**

| *Part Two - Invocations*

8. Maha Chohan, help me become aware of the spirits I have created without taking them too seriously or being burdened by it. Help me see that all of my negative feelings come from the spirits in my subconscious mind. Thus, they are not truly my feelings.

> Maha Chohan, your sacred Flame,
> what beauty in your blessed name.
> Maha Chohan, what rushing flow,
> the Spirit one with life below.
>
> **O Holy Spirit, flow through me,**
> **I am the open door for thee.**
> **O mighty rushing stream of Light,**
> **transcendence is my sacred right.**

Part 4

1. Maha Chohan, help me see that when I first took embodiment, I needed a spirit in order to integrate with the physical body. Thus, creating such spirits is a natural part of taking incarnation.

> Maha Chohan, I will to grow,
> I feel the power of your flow.
> Maha Chohan, the veil is rent,
> creative will from heaven sent.
>
> **O Holy Spirit, flow through me,**
> **I am the open door for thee.**
> **O mighty rushing stream of Light,**
> **transcendence is my sacred right.**

2. Maha Chohan, I no longer want to be identified with these spirits. I want to let them die so I can ascend to the next level of consciousness.

> Maha Chohan, your wisdom streams,
> awaken all from matter's dreams.
> Maha Chohan, your balance bring,
> let bells of integration ring.
>
> **O Holy Spirit, flow through me,**
> **I am the open door for thee.**
> **O mighty rushing stream of Light,**
> **transcendence is my sacred right.**

3. Maha Chohan, shatter the illusion that I can somehow expand or perfect a spirit, until it becomes acceptable to God.

> Maha Chohan, love's mighty call,
> the prison walls are shattered all.
> Maha Chohan, set all life free
> through unconditionality.
>
> **O Holy Spirit, flow through me,**
> **I am the open door for thee.**
> **O mighty rushing stream of Light,**
> **transcendence is my sacred right.**

4. Maha Chohan, shatter the illusion that I can enter the ascended state while being identified with a spirit, rather than entering the ascended state by giving up the very last ghost of any spirit in my lower being.

> Maha Chohan, intentions pure,
> all life is one, I know for sure.
> Maha Chohan, I am awake,
> surrender all for oneness' sake.

| *Part Two - Invocations*

**O Holy Spirit, flow through me,
I am the open door for thee.
O mighty rushing stream of Light,
transcendence is my sacred right.**

5. Maha Chohan, help me see the difference between the true inner path of self-transcendence, and the false, outer path of seeking to perfect a non-self-aware spirit created here below.

Maha Chohan, help all men see,
through veils of unreality.
Maha Chohan, with single eye,
I know I am the greater "I."

**O Holy Spirit, flow through me,
I am the open door for thee.
O mighty rushing stream of Light,
transcendence is my sacred right.**

6. Maha Chohan, help me truly know and experience, that my central ability is the ability to consciously transcend myself, my sense of self.

Maha Chohan, your peace I find,
Maitreya shows me to be kind.
Maha Chohan, all war will cease,
now flooding all with sacred peace.

**O Holy Spirit, flow through me,
I am the open door for thee.
O mighty rushing stream of Light,
transcendence is my sacred right.**

7. Maha Chohan, help me see that my sense of self is just a self, a spirit, that is not me.

> Maha Chohan, you balance all,
> the seven rays upon my call.
> Maha Chohan, all life is free,
> transcending for eternity.
>
> **O Holy Spirit, flow through me,**
> **I am the open door for thee.**
> **O mighty rushing stream of Light,**
> **transcendence is my sacred right.**

8. Maha Chohan, help me learn to consciously use my natural ability to pull myself away from my current sense of self, so I can accelerate my path to a higher level.

> Maha Chohan, your sacred Flame,
> what beauty in your blessed name.
> Maha Chohan, what rushing flow,
> the Spirit one with life below.
>
> **O Holy Spirit, flow through me,**
> **I am the open door for thee.**
> **O mighty rushing stream of Light,**
> **transcendence is my sacred right.**

Part 5

1. Maha Chohan, help me see and transcend the collective spirits from the area where I grew up, so I can claim my right to make my own choices.

> Maha Chohan, I will to grow,
> I feel the power of your flow.
> Maha Chohan, the veil is rent,
> creative will from heaven sent.

Part Two - Invocations

> O Holy Spirit, flow through me,
> I am the open door for thee.
> O mighty rushing stream of Light,
> transcendence is my sacred right.

2. Maha Chohan, help me see that I have already used the process of dis-identifying myself from a certain spirit and rising above it.

> Maha Chohan, your wisdom streams,
> awaken all from matter's dreams.
> Maha Chohan, your balance bring,
> let bells of integration ring.

> O Holy Spirit, flow through me,
> I am the open door for thee.
> O mighty rushing stream of Light,
> transcendence is my sacred right.

3. Maha Chohan, help me see and transcend the more subtle collective spirits, that are beyond outer characteristics and thus not so easy to recognize.

> Maha Chohan, love's mighty call,
> the prison walls are shattered all.
> Maha Chohan, set all life free
> through unconditionality.

> O Holy Spirit, flow through me,
> I am the open door for thee.
> O mighty rushing stream of Light,
> transcendence is my sacred right.

4. Maha Chohan, help me especially see how I have been influenced by the aggressive spirit, of wanting to prove other people wrong and wanting to prove myself right.

> Maha Chohan, intentions pure,
> all life is one, I know for sure.
> Maha Chohan, I am awake,
> surrender all for oneness' sake.
>
> **O Holy Spirit, flow through me,**
> **I am the open door for thee.**
> **O mighty rushing stream of Light,**
> **transcendence is my sacred right.**

5. Maha Chohan, help me gradually see through and transcend all of these subtle spirits, that are floating around in the collective consciousness.

> Maha Chohan, help all men see,
> through veils of unreality.
> Maha Chohan, with single eye,
> I know I am the greater "I."
>
> **O Holy Spirit, flow through me,**
> **I am the open door for thee.**
> **O mighty rushing stream of Light,**
> **transcendence is my sacred right.**

6. Maha Chohan, help me see and transcend any spirits I have become tied to or have created, as a result of my involvement with a spiritual teaching or organization.

> Maha Chohan, your peace I find,
> Maitreya shows me to be kind.
> Maha Chohan, all war will cease,
> now flooding all with sacred peace.

Part Two - Invocations

**O Holy Spirit, flow through me,
I am the open door for thee.
O mighty rushing stream of Light,
transcendence is my sacred right.**

7. Maha Chohan, help me accept that there will be some spirit I am dealing with until the moment I give up the last ghost and ascend. Thus, I need to be perpetually aware of the need to see and transcend the next spirit.

> Maha Chohan, you balance all,
> the seven rays upon my call.
> Maha Chohan, all life is free,
> transcending for eternity.

**O Holy Spirit, flow through me,
I am the open door for thee.
O mighty rushing stream of Light,
transcendence is my sacred right.**

8. Maha Chohan, I hereby accept that this is the reality of the spiritual path, and I decide to sharpen my ability to see through spirits and free myself from them.

> Maha Chohan, your sacred Flame,
> what beauty in your blessed name.
> Maha Chohan, what rushing flow,
> the Spirit one with life below.

**O Holy Spirit, flow through me,
I am the open door for thee.
O mighty rushing stream of Light,
transcendence is my sacred right.**

Part 6

1. Maha Chohan, I am willing to take responsibility and become fully aware of the process, whereby I see and dis-identify myself from a given spirit.

> Maha Chohan, I will to grow,
> I feel the power of your flow.
> Maha Chohan, the veil is rent,
> creative will from heaven sent.
>
> **O Holy Spirit, flow through me,**
> **I am the open door for thee.**
> **O mighty rushing stream of Light,**
> **transcendence is my sacred right.**

2. Maha Chohan, I am also willing to have direct, inner contact with you, so that I can be given a vision of how a certain spirit has taken individual form in me.

> Maha Chohan, your wisdom streams,
> awaken all from matter's dreams.
> Maha Chohan, your balance bring,
> let bells of integration ring.
>
> **O Holy Spirit, flow through me,**
> **I am the open door for thee.**
> **O mighty rushing stream of Light,**
> **transcendence is my sacred right.**

3. Maha Chohan, I am willing to know that I am affected by a certain spirit, and know the characteristics of that spirit.

> Maha Chohan, love's mighty call,
> the prison walls are shattered all.
> Maha Chohan, set all life free
> through unconditionality.

| *Part Two - Invocations*

**O Holy Spirit, flow through me,
I am the open door for thee.
O mighty rushing stream of Light,
transcendence is my sacred right.**

4. Maha Chohan, I take responsibility for making the shift in consciousness, whereby I pull the Conscious You outside of the spirit, so that I see the spirit from the outside, seeing that it is not me.

Maha Chohan, intentions pure,
all life is one, I know for sure.
Maha Chohan, I am awake,
surrender all for oneness' sake.

**O Holy Spirit, flow through me,
I am the open door for thee.
O mighty rushing stream of Light,
transcendence is my sacred right.**

5. Maha Chohan, I am willing to become aware of the natural ability I have, and I am willing to consciously experience pure awareness.

Maha Chohan, help all men see,
through veils of unreality.
Maha Chohan, with single eye,
I know I am the greater "I."

**O Holy Spirit, flow through me,
I am the open door for thee.
O mighty rushing stream of Light,
transcendence is my sacred right.**

6. Maha Chohan, I will not be discouraged, and I will use the tools you have given me, for diminishing the magnetic pull of my current spirit.

> Maha Chohan, your peace I find,
> Maitreya shows me to be kind.
> Maha Chohan, all war will cease,
> now flooding all with sacred peace.
>
> **O Holy Spirit, flow through me,**
> **I am the open door for thee.**
> **O mighty rushing stream of Light,**
> **transcendence is my sacred right.**

7. Maha Chohan, help me tune in to the "I will be" aspect of my being, so that I can fully feel my desire to be more and thus transcend my current spirit.

> Maha Chohan, you balance all,
> the seven rays upon my call.
> Maha Chohan, all life is free,
> transcending for eternity.
>
> **O Holy Spirit, flow through me,**
> **I am the open door for thee.**
> **O mighty rushing stream of Light,**
> **transcendence is my sacred right.**

8. Maha Chohan, help me see how this spirit has formed a magnetic pull on my attention, that keeps me trapped in focusing on certain aspects of life, that I think I cannot leave behind.

> Maha Chohan, your sacred Flame,
> what beauty in your blessed name.
> Maha Chohan, what rushing flow,
> the Spirit one with life below.

| *Part Two - Invocations*

> O Holy Spirit, flow through me,
> I am the open door for thee.
> O mighty rushing stream of Light,
> transcendence is my sacred right.

Part 7

1. Maha Chohan, help me see any spirit that aggressively seeks to keep me trapped at my current level of awareness. Help me become aware of this aggressive force and how it seeks to override my free will.

> Maha Chohan, I will to grow,
> I feel the power of your flow.
> Maha Chohan, the veil is rent,
> creative will from heaven sent.

> **O Holy Spirit, flow through me,**
> **I am the open door for thee.**
> **O mighty rushing stream of Light,**
> **transcendence is my sacred right.**

2. Maha Chohan, I am willing to see any spirit that is hiding from me. I am willing to force it out in the open, so I can see it and stop identifying myself with it.

> Maha Chohan, your wisdom streams,
> awaken all from matter's dreams.
> Maha Chohan, your balance bring,
> let bells of integration ring.

> **O Holy Spirit, flow through me,**
> **I am the open door for thee.**
> **O mighty rushing stream of Light,**
> **transcendence is my sacred right.**

3. Maha Chohan, help me see that my ego is not the same as a specific spirit, because it is more than the spirit.

Maha Chohan, love's mighty call,
the prison walls are shattered all.
Maha Chohan, set all life free
through unconditionality.

**O Holy Spirit, flow through me,
I am the open door for thee.
O mighty rushing stream of Light,
transcendence is my sacred right.**

4. Maha Chohan, help me see that the ego is beyond any given spirit, because the ego is that which keeps me in embodiment, and keeps me out of the ascended state.

Maha Chohan, intentions pure,
all life is one, I know for sure.
Maha Chohan, I am awake,
surrender all for oneness' sake.

**O Holy Spirit, flow through me,
I am the open door for thee.
O mighty rushing stream of Light,
transcendence is my sacred right.**

5. Maha Chohan, help me see that there are levels of the ego. Thus, being free of the obvious aggressive ego does not mean I am free of ego.

Maha Chohan, help all men see,
through veils of unreality.
Maha Chohan, with single eye,
I know I am the greater "I."

| *Part Two - Invocations*

**O Holy Spirit, flow through me,
I am the open door for thee.
O mighty rushing stream of Light,
transcendence is my sacred right.**

6. Maha Chohan, help me see and accept that I will not be completely free of ego until I ascend.

Maha Chohan, your peace I find,
Maitreya shows me to be kind.
Maha Chohan, all war will cease,
now flooding all with sacred peace.

**O Holy Spirit, flow through me,
I am the open door for thee.
O mighty rushing stream of Light,
transcendence is my sacred right.**

7. Maha Chohan, shatter the illusion that I can reach some ultimate level of attainment while I am still here on earth.

Maha Chohan, you balance all,
the seven rays upon my call.
Maha Chohan, all life is free,
transcending for eternity.

**O Holy Spirit, flow through me,
I am the open door for thee.
O mighty rushing stream of Light,
transcendence is my sacred right.**

8. Maha Chohan, I now consciously accept that there is always a need for self-transcendence, for self-transcendence IS life. Self-transcendence is the Holy Spirit. And life I AM. And the Holy Spirit, I AM.

Maha Chohan, your sacred Flame,
what beauty in your blessed name.
Maha Chohan, what rushing flow,
the Spirit one with life below.

**O Holy Spirit, flow through me,
I am the open door for thee.
O mighty rushing stream of Light,
transcendence is my sacred right.**

Oneness Decree

1. Surya, thou perfectly balanced one,
shining your light like a radiant sun,
from the God Star infusing the Earth
with unstoppable power, producing rebirth.

**Oh Alpha-Omega in Great Central Sun,
release now the Infinite Power of One,
to shatter the veil of duality's lies,
cutting all people free from its ties.**

**Beloved Surya, your balancing power,
flooding the Earth like a radiant shower,
as Father and Mother in oneness we see,
in infinite bliss forever we'll be.**

2. Resurrecting the feminine in woman and man,
revealing the matrix of God's perfect plan,
consuming all images graven and old,
raising religion beyond earthly mold.

| *Part Two - Invocations*

**Oh Alpha-Omega in Great Central Sun,
release now the Infinite Power of One,
to shatter the veil of duality's lies,
cutting all people free from its ties.**

**Beloved Surya, your balancing power,
flooding the Earth like a radiant shower,
as Father and Mother in oneness we see,
in infinite bliss forever we'll be.**

3. Saint Germain's Golden Age a reality at last,
the lies of duality a thing of the past,
the Mother Divine is raised up in all,
who listen within and follow the call.

**Oh Alpha-Omega in Great Central Sun,
release now the Infinite Power of One,
to shatter the veil of duality's lies,
cutting all people free from its ties.**

**Beloved Surya, your balancing power,
flooding the Earth like a radiant shower,
as Father and Mother in oneness we see,
in infinite bliss forever we'll be.**

4. Maraytaii is the name of the Mother Divine,
who calls all her children to let their light shine,
with Jesus we now take the ultimate stand,
affirming the Kingdom of God is at hand.

**Oh Alpha-Omega in Great Central Sun,
release now the Infinite Power of One,
to shatter the veil of duality's lies,
cutting all people free from its ties.**

**Beloved Surya, your balancing power,
flooding the Earth like a radiant shower,
as Father and Mother in oneness we see,
in infinite bliss forever we'll be.**

5. Mother Mary is showing all people the way,
to the kingdom within through the feminine ray,
for when we see God within every form,
we know that abundance is truly the norm.

**Oh Alpha-Omega in Great Central Sun,
release now the Infinite Power of One,
to shatter the veil of duality's lies,
cutting all people free from its ties.**

**Beloved Surya, your balancing power,
flooding the Earth like a radiant shower,
as Father and Mother in oneness we see,
in infinite bliss forever we'll be.**

6. And now we are led by the great Master MORE,
across the vast sea to a welcoming shore,
where all of duality's voices will cease,
as with the Lord Buddha we're centered in peace.

**Oh Alpha-Omega in Great Central Sun,
release now the Infinite Power of One,
to shatter the veil of duality's lies,
cutting all people free from its ties.**

**Beloved Surya, your balancing power,
flooding the Earth like a radiant shower,
as Father and Mother in oneness we see,
in infinite bliss forever we'll be.**

7. As Alpha-Omega their union reveal,
we know separation cannot be real,
and thus we can enter the Great Central Sun,
where ultimate victory of union is won.

**Oh Alpha-Omega in Great Central Sun,
release now the Infinite Power of One,
to shatter the veil of duality's lies,
cutting all people free from its ties.**

| *Part Two - Invocations*

**Beloved Surya, your balancing power,
flooding the Earth like a radiant shower,
as Father and Mother in oneness we see,
in infinite bliss forever we'll be.**

8. And thus we go forth to proclaim the great plan,
to bridge separation between God and Man.
Accepting the call co-creators to be,
as we raise the Earth to her God-victory.

**Oh Alpha-Omega in Great Central Sun,
release now the Infinite Power of One,
to shatter the veil of duality's lies,
cutting all people free from its ties.**

**Beloved Surya, your balancing power,
flooding the Earth like a radiant shower,
as Father and Mother in oneness we see,
in infinite bliss forever we'll be.**

Sealing:

In the name of the Divine Mother, I call to the seven Chohans and the Maha Chohan for the sealing of myself and all people in my circle of influence in the creative flow of the seven rays. I call for the multiplication of my calls by the entire Spirit of the Ascended Masters, so that we form the perfect figure-eight flow of "As Above, so below." Thus, I accept that this is fully manifest, because the mouth of the Lord, the Christ within me, has spoken it. Amen.

Part Three

Decree vigil

By engaging in the vigil, you will develop a good intuitive sense for the characteristics and the vibration of each ray, and you will hopefully develop an intuitive connection to at least one ascended master. This will help you unlock your creative powers in general, but it might also give you a feel for which ray you are specifically working with at the present level of your personal path.

*It is up to you how many times a day
you want to give each decree,
but as a good start,
you could give
the Archangel decree 9 times in the morning
and then give the Elohim
and the Chohan decrees 9 times
each in the evening.
Obviously, you will get more powerful results
by giving the decrees more times,
but it is important
not to turn this into a race
that might exhaust you.*

*As a practical approach,
you can decide
how much time you can spend,
for example 15 minutes
or half an hour,
and then give a decree
for that length of time
without counting.*

Introduction to the Seven-month Vigil

In Part Two of *Flowing with the River of Life* you find teachings on the seven spiritual rays, including a description of the ray, a description of the Chohan and a dictation by the Chohan. In this section you find the text for the decrees for each ray, including a decree for the Elohim, one for the Archangel and one for the Chohan of each ray. The ascended masters encourage you to engage in a vigil, where you spend one month focusing on the First Ray, then one month focusing on the Second Ray and so on, until you are familiar with all of the rays.

By engaging in this vigil, you will develop a good intuitive sense for the characteristics and the vibration of each ray, and you will hopefully develop an intuitive connection to at least one ascended master. This will help you unlock your creative powers in general, but it might also give you a feel for which ray you are specifically working with at the present level of your personal path. After the seven-month vigil, you can then spend more time on that ray, giving the decrees and invocations for the ray. You can also use the specific book for that ray and study the characteristics in greater depth.

During the one month where you focus on a specific ray, you are encouraged to study the teachings on that ray in *Flowing with the River of Life* and then use the decrees in this book. You might read a little bit from the book before you give a decree session, or you can meditate on the characteristics and perversions listed before the decrees.

It is up to you how many times a day you want to give each decree, but as a good start, you could give the Archangel decree 9 times in the morning and then give the Elohim and the Chohan decrees 9 times each in the evening. Obviously, you will get more powerful results by giving the decrees more times, but it is important not to turn this into a race that might exhaust you. As a practical approach, you can decide how much time you can spend, for example 15 minutes or half an hour, and then give a decree for that length of time without counting.

If you have purchased the E-book version of this book, you will have recordings of the decrees, so you can give them along with the recording. If you are new to decreeing, this is a good way to learn the technical aspects of decreeing and also build a momentum on invoking spiritual light. Yet you can naturally get good results from decreeing on your own, perhaps once in a while decreeing more slowly and focusing on the meaning of the words.

How to give decrees

Giving decrees is easy to do. You simply read them aloud. Obviously, if you purchased the kit with e-book and sound recordings, you can simply give the decrees along with the recordings.

Be aware that for many spiritual people, speaking a decree aloud might require a bit of an adjustment. The reason is that many of us are so used to meditating in silence. Yet once you decide to give it a sincere try, you will likely find that you quickly get used to it. The best motivation for continuing to give decrees is that you experience that they work. You will often be amazed at how much more light you can invoke through the spoken word compared to silent meditation (not to say that silent meditation is not useful; it is simply that the spoken word is a very powerful force).

WHERE DO I GIVE A DECREE?

You can do it anywhere, but most people prefer to sit in a private, quiet room, where they can remain undisturbed. Given that decrees are short, you have great flexibility in how much time you spend on them. Thus, you can easily fit them into your daily schedule whenever you have a break. Most people prefer to sit in a comfortable chair. Sit in a somewhat upright, but comfortable position. It helps the energies flow better.

WHEN DO I GIVE A DECREE?

You can give a decree any time. Some people like to give a session in the morning because the effect carries through the day and often makes your day easier. This is especially true for decrees that invoke spiritual protection, so that you are protected throughout the day. Then, in the evening you can give decrees for transmutation of lower energies and for cutting you free from whatever energies you pick up during the day.

HOW DO I READ THE DECREE?

You have the decree itself, a preamble and a sealing. The preamble invokes the Presence of the master who sponsors the decree. After the preamble, you typically give a short statement that dedicates the decree to resolving a specific issue. After that you give the body of the decree, usually several times. And finally, you give the sealing once to complete the session and seal the energies and yourself.

A decree rhymes, which means you can give it in a rhythmic manner, which invokes more light. You can indeed give a decree slowly while meditating on the words, and this is a good way to get started. You can also give a decree in a more powerful, almost staccato rhythm. And finally, you can give a decree more quickly, where it becomes a flow that almost has its own power behind it.

| *Part Three - Decree vigil*

Because a decree rhymes, it has a certain rhythm, and it is important that you learn the correct rhythm. If you purchased the kit with e-book and recordings, you can obviously use the recordings to learn the rhythm. If you purchased the printed book, go to the *www.transcendencetoolbox.com* and choose "Decrees to the seven rays." For each decree there is a sound file that will teach you the correct rhythm.

There is almost no limit to how quickly you can give a decree, and experienced practitioners can give a decree so quickly that inexperienced people simply cannot hear the words. However, a decree is only effective when you engage your heart chakra, and thus it is more important to feel your heart being engaged than giving a decree quickly.

You typically give a decree several times. The ascended masters say that there are certain numbers that allow them to multiply the effect of a decree. These numbers are 3 times, 9 times, 24 times and 36 times.

THE FIRST RAY

Color: **Electric blue**
Corresponding chakra: **Throat**

Elohim and their retreat:
Hercules and Amazonia
Half Dome, Sierra Nevada, California, U.S.A.

Archangel, Archeia and their retreat:
Michael and Faith
Banff and Lake Louise, Canada

Chohan and his retreat:
Master MORE, also known as El Morya, Morya, Master M, M, or Bapu.
Darjeeling, India

Part Three - Decree vigil

PURE QUALITIES OF THE FIRST RAY

- The drive to be MORE and desire for self-transcendence.
- The will to express yourself.
- Flowing with the River of Life, which is constant self-transcendence.
- The will and the intent to expand self-awareness by expressing one's creative abilities.
- Using power to produce a change that enhances life.
- The will to learn about yourself by seeing the result of what you created.
- The innocence of the will to experiment.
- The will to transcend your current state of consciousness.
- The will to seek mastery of mind over matter.
- The will to seek a balanced expression of creativity that raises life.
- Honesty.
- Taking full responsibility for yourself.
- Complete respect for the free will of yourself and others.
- Seeking to inspire others to self-transcend out of a free choice.
- Working to bring forth new ideas that help people and societies transcend.
- Always being open to a higher idea.
- Being balanced in all expressions, seeking the Middle Way instead of going into extremes.
- Never struggling against other people, but always working towards a positive, non-violent goal.
- The desire to affect positive change, to make a difference.
- Will to speak out against and expose the misuse of power.
- Doing right action while being non-attached to the fruits of action.
- Being non-attached to producing a specific result but seeking to raise all life.
- Seeking to raise people's awareness instead of producing physical results.

- Looking for solutions that are not based on the force-based mindset but on the infinite creativity of God.
- The willingness to transcend your current state of consciousness in order to be the open door for ideas that you cannot see right now.
- The willingness to act, to do something. Yet acting without using force, but finding the Middle Way to act without dualistic force but with the power of God.

| *Part Three - Decree vigil*

1.01 Decree to Hercules and Amazonia

In the name I AM THAT I AM, Jesus Christ, I call to my I AM Presence to flow through the I Will Be Presence that I AM and give these decrees with full power. I call to beloved Mighty Hercules and Amazonia to release flood tides of electric blue light, to protect me from all imperfect energies and dark forces, including…

[Make personal calls]

    1. O Hercules Blue, you fill every space,
with infinite Power and infinite Grace,
you embody the key to creativity,
the will to transcend into Infinity.

**O Hercules Blue, in oneness with thee,
I open my heart to your reality,
in feeling your flame, so clearly I see,
transcending my self is the true alchemy.**

    2. O Hercules Blue, I lovingly raise,
my voice in giving God infinite praise,
I'm grateful for playing my personal part,
In God's infinitely intricate work of art.

**O Hercules Blue, all life now you heal,
enveloping all in your Blue-flame Seal,
your electric-blue fire within us reveal,
our innermost longing for all that is real.**

    3. O Hercules Blue, I pledge now my life,
in helping this planet transcend human strife,
duality's lies are pierced by your light,
restoring the fullness of my inner sight.

O Hercules Blue, I'm one with your will,
all space in my being with Blue Flame you fill,
your power allows me to forge on until,
I pierce every veil and climb every hill.

4. O Hercules Blue, your Temple of Light,
revealed to us all through our inner sight,
a beacon that radiates light to the Earth,
bringing about our planet's rebirth.

O Hercules Blue, all life you defend,
giving us power to always transcend,
in you the expansion of self has no end,
as I in God's infinite spirals ascend.

Coda:

Accelerate into Creativity, I AM real,
Accelerate into Creativity, all life heal,
Accelerate into Creativity, I AM MORE,
Accelerate into Creativity, all will soar.

Accelerate into Creativity! (3X)
Beloved Hercules and Amazonia.

Accelerate into Creativity! (3X)
Beloved Michael and Faith.

Accelerate into Creativity! (3X)
Beloved Master MORE.

Accelerate into Creativity! (3X)
Beloved I AM.

Sealing:

In the name of the Divine Mother, I fully accept that the power of these calls is used to set free the Ma-ter light, so it can outpicture the perfect vision of Christ for my own life, for all people and for the planet. In the name I AM THAT I AM, it is done! Amen.

| *Part Three - Decree vigil*

1.02 Decree to Archangel Michael

In the name I AM THAT I AM, Jesus Christ, I call to my I AM Presence to flow through the I Will Be Presence that I AM and give these decrees with full power. I call to beloved Archangel Michael and Faith to shield me in your wings of electric blue light, and shatter and consume all imperfect energies and dark forces, including…

[Make personal calls]

1. Michael Archangel, in your flame so blue,
there is no more night, there is only you.
In oneness with you, I am filled with your light,
what glorious wonder, revealed to my sight.

**Michael Archangel, your Faith is so strong,
Michael Archangel, oh sweep me along.
Michael Archangel, I'm singing your song,
Michael Archangel, with you I belong.**

2. Michael Archangel, protection you give,
within your blue shield, I ever shall live.
Sealed from all creatures, roaming the night,
I remain in your sphere, of electric blue light.

**Michael Archangel, your Faith is so strong,
Michael Archangel, oh sweep me along.
Michael Archangel, I'm singing your song,
Michael Archangel, with you I belong.**

3. Michael Archangel, what power you bring,
as millions of angels, praises will sing.
Consuming the demons, of doubt and of fear,
I know that your Presence, will always be near.

**Michael Archangel, your Faith is so strong,
Michael Archangel, oh sweep me along.
Michael Archangel, I'm singing your song,
Michael Archangel, with you I belong.**

4. Michael Archangel, God's will is your love,
you bring to us all, God's light from Above.
God's will is to see, all life taking flight,
transcendence of self, our most sacred right.

**Michael Archangel, your Faith is so strong,
Michael Archangel, oh sweep me along.
Michael Archangel, I'm singing your song,
Michael Archangel, with you I belong.**

Coda:

With angels I soar,
as I reach for MORE.
The angels so real,
their love all will heal.
The angels bring peace,
all conflicts will cease.
With angels of light,
we soar to new height.

**The rustling sound of angel wings,
what joy as even matter sings,
what joy as every atom rings,
in harmony with angel wings.**

Sealing:

In the name of the Divine Mother, I fully accept that the power of these calls is used to set free the Ma-ter light, so it can outpicture the perfect vision of Christ for my own life, for all people and for the planet. In the name I AM THAT I AM, it is done! Amen.

PERVERSIONS OF THE FIRST RAY

- The desire to be in control or to hold on, to possess.
- Stop self-transcendence by freezing the River of Life.
- The value judgment that some products of creativity right and some wrong.
- Fear of failure and and unwillingness to experiment unless there is guarantee the result will be right.
- The unwillingness to transcend, seeking to hold on to your current sense of self.
- Anarchy, the desire to create an uncontrolled explosion that blows things apart.
- The desire to have the power to destroy.
- The dishonesty of denying that you are responsible for what you have created.
- Saying that God is responsible or that God created your misery as an unjust punishment.
- Denial of your own free will in victim consciousness.
- Seeking to take away or control the free will of others.
- The unwillingness to raise up life and the desire to raise up the separate self.
- The desire to raise oneself in comparison to others and the desire to punish a scapegoat.
- A well-meaning desire to work for the greater good expressed as the need to forcefully control the will of others.
- Seeking to raise up one idea as the ultimate truth and battling against all other ideas.
- Create an epic scenario where some ultimate calamity will happen unless other people are forced to conform to your belief system.
- Taking extreme measures, because the ends can justify the means.
- Always seeking to force other people in an ongoing power struggle.

- Thinking that the way you look at things right now is the ultimate way, thus closing your mind to a higher vision.
- Willingness to kill others for some cause. War is perversion of the first ray.
- Anti-will based on a divided vision. The anti-will is opposed tot he unifying will of God that seek to raise all. Anti-will divides into right an wrong and then seeks to destroy or put down what it labels as wrong.
- Thinking there must always be opposing factions, choosing one as right and fighting the one that you see as wrong.
- Unwillingness to do anything or to try anything new.
- Clinging to what one knows, even though it has been proven not to work or not to solve current problems.

1.03 Decree to Master MORE

In the name I AM THAT I AM, Jesus Christ, I call to my I Will Be Presence to flow through my being and give these decrees with full power. I call to beloved Master MORE, the other Chohans and the Maha Chohan to release flood tides of light, to consume all blocks and attachments that prevent me from becoming one with the eternal flow of the first ray of creative will and ever-transcending power, including…

[Make personal calls]

1. Master MORE, come to the fore,
I will absorb your flame of MORE.
Master MORE, my will so strong,
my power center cleared by song.

**O Holy Spirit, flow through me,
I am the open door for thee.
O mighty rushing stream of Light,
transcendence is my sacred right.**

2. Master MORE, your wisdom flows,
as my attunement ever grows.
Master MORE, we have a tie,
that helps me see through Serpent's lie.

**O Holy Spirit, flow through me,
I am the open door for thee.
O mighty rushing stream of Light,
transcendence is my sacred right.**

3. Master MORE, your love so pink,
there is no purer love, I think.
Master MORE, you set me free,
from all conditionality.

**O Holy Spirit, flow through me,
I am the open door for thee.
O mighty rushing stream of Light,
transcendence is my sacred right.**

4. Master MORE, I will endure,
your discipline that makes me pure.
Master MORE, intentions true,
as I am always one with you.

**O Holy Spirit, flow through me,
I am the open door for thee.
O mighty rushing stream of Light,
transcendence is my sacred right.**

5. Master MORE, my vision raised,
the will of God is always praised.
Master MORE, creative will,
raising all life higher still.

**O Holy Spirit, flow through me,
I am the open door for thee.
O mighty rushing stream of Light,
transcendence is my sacred right.**

6. Master MORE, your peace is power,
the demons of war it will devour.
Master MORE, we serve all life,
our flames consuming war and strife.

**O Holy Spirit, flow through me,
I am the open door for thee.
O mighty rushing stream of Light,
transcendence is my sacred right.**

7. Master MORE, I am so free,
eternal bond from you to me.
Master MORE, I find rebirth,
in flow of your eternal mirth.

**O Holy Spirit, flow through me,
I am the open door for thee.
O mighty rushing stream of Light,
transcendence is my sacred right.**

8. Master MORE, you balance all,
the seven rays upon my call.
Master MORE, forever MORE,
I am the Spirit's open door.

**O Holy Spirit, flow through me,
I am the open door for thee.
O mighty rushing stream of Light,
transcendence is my sacred right.**

| *Part Three - Decree vigil*

Sealing:

In the name of the Divine Mother, I fully accept that the power of these calls is used to set free the Ma-ter light, so it can outpicture the perfect vision of Christ for my own life, for all people and for the planet. In the name I AM THAT I AM, it is done! Amen.

The Second Ray

Color: **Golden yellow**
Corresponding chakra: **Crown**

Elohim and their retreat:
Apollo and Lumina
Western Lower Saxony, Germany

Archangel, Archeia and their retreat:
Jophiel and Christine
South of the Great Wall near Lanchow, North Central China

Chohan and his retreat:
Lord Lanto
Grand Teton, Teton Range, Wyoming, U.S.A.

PURE QUALITIES OF THE SECOND RAY

- Willingness to experiment and learn from whatever the result.
- Open-ended drive to learn and to expand awareness.
- Self-observation based on the Christ standard beyond dualistic value judgments.
- Willingness to reach beyond mental box for true wisdom of Christ mind.
- Striving for wholeness, true wisdom and self-sufficiency through the Christ mind.
- Being willing to connect your mind to the one mind of Christ that is the fount of wisdom.
- Seeking gnosis instead of seeking to know from a distance.
- Willingness to integrate spiritual knowledge by shifting your total state of consciousness.
- Acknowledging that you must shift your consciousness in order to enter heaven.
- Seeking true oneness with the Spirit of Wisdom.
- Knowing that God has given you free will to experiment without defining an external standard.
- Knowing no one is beyond redemption and seeking to inspire all to self-transcend.
- Seeing that a given consequence is a result of your state of consciousness, thus being willing to shift your level of consciousness upwards.
- Realizing the specific consequences are not important and instead seeking to shift your sense of self.
- Knowing divine wisdom has no material proof and then seeking for inner proof through gnosis.
- Realizing that divine wisdom is always above a certain level of vibration and thus cannot be falsified by the mind of anti-christ or fit into an earthly standard.
- Being open to new ideas and thought systems, using them to raise consciousness and challenge one's mental box.

- Remaining curious and always asking questions that go beyond "established wisdom " or one's personal mental box.
- The willingness to reach beyond thought and experience pure awareness.
- Seeking non-linear, spherical wisdom that is beyond words and thought systems.
- Realizing wisdom is always transcending itself.
- Seeing that any thought system is based on a certain level of consciousness, so if we don't reach beyond it, we will keep ourselves at that level of consciousness.
- Realizing that as consciousness is raised, mind can transcend the laws of matter.
- Realizing the highest wisdom that everything is an expression of consciousness.
- Throwing yourself into the river of living wisdom instead of seeking to know it from the outside.
- Always a need to challenge the thought system that keeps people's minds in a closed box.
- Looking at reality without wanting it to validate currents world view.
- Being willing to see that currently all thought systems are affected by the duality consciousness, and thus all of them must be transcended.
- Seeking freedom of mind to flow with the living waters of wisdom.
- Evaluating whether ideas can answer your questions and whether they resonate with the inner core of your being.
- Seeking to become an open door fro bringing forth new ideas that will take any debate to a higher level.
- Being willing to open the mind to go beyond all preconceived opinions and receive new ideas.
- Realizing the need to look at a problem from a greater perspective instead of looking at it from inside the consciousness that precipitated the problem.
- Seeking gnosis in seeking to unite your mind with the consciousness behind any form.

| *Part Three - Decree vigil*

2.01 Decree to Apollo and Lumina

In the name I AM THAT I AM, Jesus Christ, I call to my I Will Be Presence to flow through my being and give these decrees with full power. I call to beloved Mighty Apollo and Lumina to release flood tides of Wisdom's Golden Light to help us see through the most subtle deceptions of dualistic forces, including…

[Make personal calls]

>1. Beloved Apollo, with your second ray,
>you open my eyes to see a new day,
>I see through duality's lies and deceit,
>transcending the mindset producing defeat.
>
>**Beloved Apollo, thou Elohim Gold,**
>**your radiant light my eyes now behold,**
>**as pages of wisdom you gently unfold,**
>**I feel I am free from all that is old.**
>
>2. Beloved Apollo, in your flame I know,
>that your living wisdom is always a flow,
>in your light I see my own highest will,
>immersed in the stream that never stands still.
>
>**Beloved Apollo, your light makes it clear,**
>**why we have taken embodiment here,**
>**working to raise our own cosmic sphere,**
>**together we form the tip of the spear.**
>
>3. Beloved Apollo, exposing all lies,
>I hereby surrender all ego-based ties,
>I know my perception is truly the key,
>to transcending the serpentine duality.

**Beloved Apollo, we heed now your call,
drawing us into Wisdom's Great Hall,
exposing all lies causing the fall,
you help us reclaim the oneness of all.**

4. Beloved Apollo, your wisdom so clear,
in oneness with you, no serpent I fear,
the beam in my eye I'm willing to see,
I'm free from the serpent's own duality.

**Beloved Apollo, my eyes now I raise,
I see that the Earth is in a new phase,
I willingly stand in your piercing gaze,
empowered, I exit duality's maze.**

Coda:

Accelerate my Awakeness, I AM real,
Accelerate my Awakeness, all life heal,
Accelerate my Awakeness, I AM MORE,
Accelerate my Awakeness, all will soar.

Accelerate my Awakeness! (3X)
Beloved Apollo and Lumina.

Accelerate my Awakeness! (3X)
Beloved Jophiel and Christine.

Accelerate my Awakeness! (3X)
Beloved Master Lanto.

Accelerate my Awakeness! (3X)
Beloved I AM.

Sealing:

In the name of the Divine Mother, I fully accept that the power of these calls is used to set free the Ma-ter light, so it can outpicture the perfect vision of Christ for my own life, for all people and for the planet. In the name I AM THAT I AM, it is done! Amen.

2.02 Decree to Archangel Jophiel

In the name I AM THAT I AM, Jesus Christ, I call to my I AM Presence to flow through the I Will Be Presence that I AM and give these decrees with full power. I call to beloved Archangel Jophiel and Christine to shield me in your wings of golden yellow light, and shatter and consume all serpentine lies and dualistic illusions, including…

[Make personal calls]

1. Jophiel Archangel, in wisdom's great light,
all serpentine lies exposed to my sight.
So subtle the lies that creep through the mind,
yet you are the greatest teacher I find.

Jophiel Archangel, exposing all lies,
Jophiel Archangel, cutting all ties.
Jophiel Archangel, clearing the skies,
Jophiel Archangel, my mind truly flies.

2. Jophiel Archangel, your wisdom I hail,
your sword cutting through duality's veil.
As you show the way, I know what is real,
from serpentine doubt, I instantly heal.

Jophiel Archangel, exposing all lies,
Jophiel Archangel, cutting all ties.
Jophiel Archangel, clearing the skies,
Jophiel Archangel, my mind truly flies.

3. Jophiel Archangel, your reality,
the best antidote to duality.
No lie can remain in your Presence so clear,
with you on my side, no serpent I fear.

**Jophiel Archangel, exposing all lies,
Jophiel Archangel, cutting all ties.
Jophiel Archangel, clearing the skies,
Jophiel Archangel, my mind truly flies.**

4. Jophiel Archangel, God's mind is in me,
and through your clear light, its wisdom I see.
Divisions all vanish, as I see the One,
and truly, the wholeness of mind I have won.

**Jophiel Archangel, exposing all lies,
Jophiel Archangel, cutting all ties.
Jophiel Archangel, clearing the skies,
Jophiel Archangel, my mind truly flies.**

Coda:

With angels I soar,
as I reach for MORE.
The angels so real,
their love all will heal.
The angels bring peace,
all conflicts will cease.
With angels of light,
we soar to new height.

**The rustling sound of angel wings,
what joy as even matter sings,
what joy as every atom rings,
in harmony with angel wings.**

Sealing:

In the name of the Divine Mother, I fully accept that the power of these calls is used to set free the Ma-ter light, so it can outpicture the perfect vision of Christ for my own life, for all people and for the planet. In the name I AM THAT I AM, it is done! Amen.

Perversions of the Second Ray

- False wisdom compares everything to a standard of right and wrong and seeking to avoid doing what is wrong rather than experimenting.
- Feeling you know God based on an image made from the consciousness of separation and the longing for the cessation of consciousness.
- Unwillingness to evaluate consequences of your actions and willingness to ignore, or suppress, or deny curiosity.
- Thinking wisdom is comparing everything to a standard defined by mind of anti-christ or thinking you are not complete within yourself so need external authority to tell what is true.
- Thinking wisdom is knowing an external standard or thinking that intellectual knowledge is the same as wisdom or thinking you can know from a distance, you can know through a mental image rather than gnosis.
- Seeking intellectual understanding of the outer teaching while refusing gnosis with the spiritual being and seeking to always be right in a discussion while seeking to prove others wrong.
- Thinking you can get into heaven by following an outer, intellectual standard or set of rules and seeking to be thought wise among men.
- Thinking God has created the standard although it is actually created by the mind of anti-christ and wanting to judge and condemn others as being beyond redemption according to your standard.
- Defining a result as the consequence of external factors, thus denying the need to shift your state of consciousness.
- Focusing on specific consequences and judging yourself or others by them and thinking that divine wisdom should have material proof.
- Holding on to a thought system even though it has lost its explanatory power.

- Defining two competing thought systems that are both products of the false wisdom of anti-christ. Thus, the struggle between them only serves to keep people trapped in the consciousness of death.
- The privilege of formulating the problem so any outcome supports a predefined goal of keeping people blinded by the duality consciousness.
- The belief that the mind is only thought and there is nothing beyond thought, arguing endlessly without ever coming to any final conclusion.
- Wanting to analyze every problem, thinking there must be a solution that can be found through analysis and linear knowledge.
- Thinking there must be a fixed and ultimate truth or that you have to be loyal to an earthy thought system and using the powers of the mind to deny "the mind has power over matter."
- Letting the ego use a thought system in its never-ending quest for ultimate security and looking only at evidence that confirms one's assumptions, that validates what one wants to be true.
- Insisting that subject and object will always be separate and being unable to determine what is real and unreal, for everything is subject to argumentation.

2.03 Decree to Master Lanto

In the name I AM THAT I AM, Jesus Christ, I call to my I AM Presence to flow through the I Will Be Presence that I AM and give these decrees with full power. I call to beloved Master Lanto, the other Chohans and the Maha Chohan to release flood tides of light, to consume all blocks and attachments that prevent me from becoming one with the eternal flow of the second ray of creative wisdom and ever-transcending reality, including...

[Make personal calls]

1. Master Lanto, golden wise,
expose in me the ego's lies.
Master Lanto, will to be,
I will to win my mastery.

**O Holy Spirit, flow through me,
I am the open door for thee.
O mighty rushing stream of Light,
transcendence is my sacred right.**

2. Master Lanto, balance all,
for wisdom's balance I do call.
Master Lanto, help me see,
that balance is the Golden key.

**O Holy Spirit, flow through me,
I am the open door for thee.
O mighty rushing stream of Light,
transcendence is my sacred right.**

3. Master Lanto, from Above,
I call forth discerning love.
Master Lanto, love's not blind,
through love, God vision I will find.

**O Holy Spirit, flow through me,
I am the open door for thee.
O mighty rushing stream of Light,
transcendence is my sacred right.**

4. Master Lanto, pure I am,
intentions pure as Christic lamb.
Master Lanto, I will transcend,
acceleration now my truest friend.

**O Holy Spirit, flow through me,
I am the open door for thee.
O mighty rushing stream of Light,
transcendence is my sacred right.**

5. Master Lanto, I am whole,
no more division in my soul.
Master Lanto, healing flame,
all balance in your sacred name.

**O Holy Spirit, flow through me,
I am the open door for thee.
O mighty rushing stream of Light,
transcendence is my sacred right.**

6. Master Lanto, serve all life,
as I transcend all inner strife.
Master Lanto, peace you give,
to all who want to truly live.

**O Holy Spirit, flow through me,
I am the open door for thee.
O mighty rushing stream of Light,
transcendence is my sacred right.**

7. Master Lanto, free to be,
in balanced creativity.
Master Lanto, we employ,
your balance as the key to joy.

**O Holy Spirit, flow through me,
I am the open door for thee.
O mighty rushing stream of Light,
transcendence is my sacred right.**

8. Master Lanto, balance all,
the seven rays upon my call.
Master Lanto, I take flight,
my threefold flame a blazing light.

**O Holy Spirit, flow through me,
I am the open door for thee.
O mighty rushing stream of Light,
transcendence is my sacred right.**

| *Part Three - Decree vigil*

Sealing:

In the name of the Divine Mother, I fully accept that the power of these calls is used to set free the Ma-ter light, so it can outpicture the perfect vision of Christ for my own life, for all people and for the planet. In the name I AM THAT I AM, it is done! Amen.

THE THIRD RAY

Color: **Pink**

Corresponding chakra: **Heart**

Elohim and their retreat:
Heros and Amora
Lake Winnipeg, Canada

Archangel, Archeia and their retreat:
Chamuel and Charity
St. Louise, Missouri, U.S.A.

Chohan and his retreat:
Paul the Venetian
Southern France Temple of the Sun, New York City

PURE QUALITIES OF THE THIRD RAY

- Love for self-transcendence.
- Wanting to see all life express its highest potential.
- Transcending your sense of self until you reach the level of self-awareness of a Creator.
- Acknowledging that no condition prevents you from taking the next step.
- Recognizing that while forms are defined by conditions, you are more than form, and thus you can never be defined by or trapped in any form, any sense of self.
- The desire to be the open door for the flow of love, that no condition can shut or distort.
- Knowing that God's love is beyond any conditions that can be defined in the world of form.
- Knowing God has given you free will, so nothing you can do would cause you to lose or be unworthy of God's non-conditional love.
- Knowing you could never do anything that causes you to lose the potential to transcend your former choices.
- Knowing it is God's good pleasure to give you the kingdom.
- Knowing you can always come back to righteousness and experience God's love.
- Knowing God's love is constantly being extended to all self-aware beings, regardless of how low is their state of consciousness.
- Knowing that the Conscious You has not been changed by your current sense of self, so you can at any time step outside that self and receive God's love.
- Knowing that no external conditions block yoru experience of God's love; only your sense of self blocks yu from accepting that love.
- Determination to not allow fallen consciousness to define your sense of self.
- The drive to transcend your current level of consciousness.

- Knowing you can never own or control love because love is the very force that empowers you to transcend conditions—and thus it is always beyond any conditions.
- Knowing you can be an open door for God's love, but only when you let go of all conditions.
- Allowing God to express itself through you as it sees fit.
- Realizing love is not always soft, but also the determined love that will not accept conditions that limit people's self-transcendence.
- Being open to shock people if that is necessary to help them become unstuck.
- Love for something higher than dualistic wisdom and the desire to be right according to an earthly scale.
- Loving your higher potential more than what you have right now.
- Loving your higher self so much that you are willing to let any lower sense of self die.
- Knowing that God's love has no opposite because it is not dualistic; it transcends conditions.
- Having relationships in which you set other people free to be who they are.
- Setting yourself free to be who you are, so you do not need validation from this world because you have it from your I AM Presence.
- Willing to look beyond current conditions and reach for higher potential while being non-attached to what is manifest right now.
- Knowing that in God's love there are no conditions, which means there can be no opposites.
- Seeing love as a flowing stream.
- Experiencing love and spontaneously transcending the struggle.

| *Part Three - Decree vigil*

3.01 DECREE TO HEROS AND AMORA

In the name I AM THAT I AM, Jesus Christ, I call to my I Will Be Presence to flow through my being and give these decrees with full power. I call to beloved Heros and Amora to release flood tides of Love's Ruby-Pink Fire, to consume in me all conditions that separate me from the River of Life, including…

[Make personal calls]

1. O Heros-Amora, in your love so pink,
I care not what others about me may think,
in oneness with you, I claim a new day,
an innocent child, I frolic and play.

**O Heros-Amora, a new life begun,
I laugh at the devil, the serious one,
I bathe in your glorious Ruby-Pink Sun,
knowing my God allows life to be fun.**

2. O Heros-Amora, life is such a joy,
I see that the world is like a great toy,
whatever my mind into it projects,
the mirror of life exactly reflects.

**O Heros-Amora, I reap what I sow,
yet this is Plan B for helping me grow,
for truly, Plan A is that I join the flow,
immersed in the Infinite Love you bestow.**

3. O Heros-Amora, conditions you burn,
I know I AM free to take a new turn,
Immersed in the stream of infinite Love,
I know that my Spirit came from Above.

O Heros-Amora, awakened I see,
in true love is no conditionality,
the devil is stuck in his duality,
but I AM set free by Love's reality.

4. O Heros-Amora, I feel that at last,
I've risen above the trap of my past,
in true love I claim my freedom to grow,
forever I'm one with Love's Infinite Flow.

O Heros-Amora, conditions are ties,
forming a net of serpentine lies,
your love has no bounds, forever it flies,
raising all life into Ruby-Pink skies.

Coda:

Accelerate into Oneness, I AM real,
Accelerate into Oneness, all life heal,
Accelerate into Oneness, I AM MORE,
Accelerate into Oneness, all will soar.

Accelerate into Oneness! (3X)
Beloved Heros and Amora.

Accelerate into Oneness! (3X)
Beloved Chamuel and Charity.

Accelerate into Oneness! (3X)
Beloved Paul the Venetian.

Accelerate into Oneness! (3X)
Beloved I AM.

Sealing:

In the name of the Divine Mother, I fully accept that the power of these calls is used to set free the Ma-ter light, so it can outpicture the perfect vision of Christ for my own life, for all people and for the planet. In the name I AM THAT I AM, it is done! Amen.

| *Part Three - Decree vigil*

3.02 Decree to Archangel Chamuel

In the name I AM THAT I AM, Jesus Christ, I call to my I AM Presence to flow through the I Will Be Presence that I AM and give these decrees with full power. I call to beloved Archangel Chamuel and Charity to shield me in your wings of ruby pink light, and shatter and consume all imperfect energies and dark forces, including…

[Make personal calls]

1. Chamuel Archangel, in ruby ray power,
I know I am taking a life-giving shower.
Love burning away all perversions of will,
I suddenly feel my desires falling still

**Chamuel Archangel, descend from Above,
Chamuel Archangel, with ruby-pink love,
Chamuel Archangel, so often thought-of,
Chamuel Archangel, o come Holy Dove.**

2. Chamuel Archangel, a spiral of light,
as ruby ray fire now pierces the night.
All forces of darkness consumed by your fire,
consuming all those who will not rise higher.

**Chamuel Archangel, descend from Above,
Chamuel Archangel, with ruby-pink love,
Chamuel Archangel, so often thought-of,
Chamuel Archangel, o come Holy Dove.**

3. Chamuel Archangel, your love so immense,
with clarified vision, my life now makes sense.
The purpose of life you so clearly reveal,
immersed in your love, God's oneness I feel.

**Chamuel Archangel, descend from Above,
Chamuel Archangel, with ruby-pink love,
Chamuel Archangel, so often thought-of,
Chamuel Archangel, o come Holy Dove.**

4. Chamuel Archangel, what calmness you bring,
I see now that even death has no sting.
For truly, in love there can be no decay,
as love is transcendence into a new day.

**Chamuel Archangel, descend from Above,
Chamuel Archangel, with ruby-pink love,
Chamuel Archangel, so often thought-of,
Chamuel Archangel, o come Holy Dove.**

Coda:

With angels I soar,
as I reach for MORE.
The angels so real,
their love all will heal.
The angels bring peace,
all conflicts will cease.
With angels of light,
we soar to new height.

**The rustling sound of angel wings,
what joy as even matter sings,
what joy as every atom rings,
in harmony with angel wings.**

Sealing:

In the name of the Divine Mother, I fully accept that the power of these calls is used to set free the Ma-ter light, so it can outpicture the perfect vision of Christ for my own life, for all people and for the planet. In the name I AM THAT I AM, it is done! Amen.

Perversions of the Third Ray

- Possessive love that seeks to control the object of love or love based on changing conditions or personal idiosyncrasies.
- Wanting to reduce everything to something that can be quantified and thus becomes predictable and the desire to reduce love to something that can be grasped by the outer, intellectual, linear mind.
- Wanting to control the future and limit the options for what can happen, a vision of what should or should not happen based on a perspective centered around the separate self.
- Thinking you are above other people, that you are a god on earth who can get away with anything and wanting to have the status, power and privileges of a god without transcending the separate self.
- Accepting conditions in this world that limit how you can express love and defining a scale that says some people are not worthy of love, even God's love.
- Thinking you can make choices that you cannot transcend by making better choices.
- Thinking you have done something so bd you can never again be acceptable to God.
- Actively rejecting God's love by projecting a negative image upon God, saying God is the one withholding love from you.
- Identifying yourself based on what you have done or not done on earth.
- Thinking that giving and receiving love depends on external conditions and thinking that you can own or control love based on dualistic, self-centered, perverted conditions.
- Thinking love is yours to give or withhold.
- Human love as a psychic projection to control other people.
- Thinking you own other people because you have deemed them worthy of your love.
- Thinking love is always soft and accepts people for who they are.

- Judging yourself and others based on your standard that defines love.
- Thinking God expresses love based on your standard and thus you can decide when God withholds love from other people.
- Claiming to love someone else while in reality loving something – a feeling or world view – inside oneself.
- Loving only the separate self and the role it defines. being willing to sacrifice anything or anyone in order to maintain that image.
- Holding on to what you have right now as if it was the ultimate level.
- Loving a graven image and worshiping it as the ultimate god.
- Thinking love is the opposite of fear or hatred, while failing to see that this is dualistic love, conditional love.
- Love-hate relationships.
- Seeing yourself as set apart from all other people, thus hating all people who will not confirm your self-image.
- Loving the epic battle and the sense that one is superior compared to the scapegoat, those that the epic image labels as evil.
- Loving the opposites and the conditions that define them.
- Loving the struggle against opponents.

3.03 Decree to Paul the Venetian

In the name I AM THAT I AM, Jesus Christ, I call to my I AM Presence to flow through the I Will Be Presence that I AM and give these decrees with full power. I call to beloved Paul the Venetian, the other Chohans and the Maha Chohan to release flood tides of light, to consume all blocks and attachments that prevent me from becoming one with the eternal flow of the third ray of creative love and ever-transcending oneness, including…

[Make personal calls]

1. Master Paul, venetian dream,
your love for beauty's flowing stream.
Master Paul, in love's own womb,
your power shatters ego's tomb.

**O Holy Spirit, flow through me,
I am the open door for thee.
O mighty rushing stream of Light,
transcendence is my sacred right.**

2. Master Paul, your counsel wise,
my mind is raised to lofty skies.
Master Paul, in wisdom's love,
such beauty flowing from Above.

**O Holy Spirit, flow through me,
I am the open door for thee.
O mighty rushing stream of Light,
transcendence is my sacred right.**

3. Master Paul, love is an art,
it opens up the secret heart.
Master Paul, love's rushing flow,
my heart awash in sacred glow.

**O Holy Spirit, flow through me,
I am the open door for thee.
O mighty rushing stream of Light,
transcendence is my sacred right.**

4. Master Paul, accelerate,
upon pure love I meditate.
Master Paul, intentions pure,
my self-transcendence will ensure.

**O Holy Spirit, flow through me,
I am the open door for thee.
O mighty rushing stream of Light,
transcendence is my sacred right.**

5. Master Paul, your love will heal,
my inner light you do reveal.
Master Paul, all life console,
with you I'm being truly whole.

**O Holy Spirit, flow through me,
I am the open door for thee.
O mighty rushing stream of Light,
transcendence is my sacred right.**

6. Master Paul, you serve the All,
by helping us transcend the fall.
Master Paul, in peace we rise,
as ego meets its sure demise.

**O Holy Spirit, flow through me,
I am the open door for thee.
O mighty rushing stream of Light,
transcendence is my sacred right.**

7. Master Paul, love all life free,
your love is for eternity.
Master Paul, you are the One,
to help us make the journey fun.

**O Holy Spirit, flow through me,
I am the open door for thee.
O mighty rushing stream of Light,
transcendence is my sacred right.**

8. Master Paul, you balance all,
the seven rays upon my call.
Master Paul, you paint the sky,
with colors that delight the I.

**O Holy Spirit, flow through me,
I am the open door for thee.
O mighty rushing stream of Light,
transcendence is my sacred right.**

| *Part Three - Decree vigil*

Sealing:

In the name of the Divine Mother, I fully accept that the power of these calls is used to set free the Ma-ter light, so it can outpicture the perfect vision of Christ for my own life, for all people and for the planet. In the name I AM THAT I AM, it is done! Amen.

The Fourth Ray

Color: **Brilliant white**
Corresponding chakra: **Base**

Elohim and their retreat:
Purity and Astrea
Near Gulf of Archangel, southeast arm of White Sea, Russia

Archangel, Archeia and their retreat:
Gabriel and Hope
Between Sacramento and Mount Shasta, California, U.S.A.

Chohan and his retreat:
Serapis Bey
Luxor, Egypt

| *Part Three - Decree vigil*

PURE QUALITIES OF THE FOURTH RAY

- Knowing that true purity is beyond any conditions defined by a dualistic thought system.
- Realizing purity is a vibration and being willing to raise your consciousness to the level of purity.
- Being willing to always accelerate oneself beyond one's current level of consciousness.
- Having balance between the love, wisdom and power of the first three rays.
- Accelerating your intent away from seeking to raise yourself as an individual, instead seeking to raise the All.
- Realizing that Christ is the principle that balances the individual self with the whole.
- Seeing the underlying connection between all beings, realizing every being springs from the same source.
- Knowing that everything is consciousness, thus every manifestation is the expression of a certain matrix of consciousness.
- Seeking to raise the self by serving the All.
- Knowing there is no comparison or value judgment in the Christ mind.
- Seeing that the attempt to define a standard fro what is pure and impure springs from the duality consciousness.
- Realizing that the real solutions to all problems is to transcend the matrix of consciousness that manifested a given condition.
- Seeing the greater perspective of the All, the Christ perspective.
- Realizing that the true solution to all problems is the Christ consciousness, which is beyond any system.
- Realizing that the only true solution is the acceleration of consciousness, individual and collective.
- Knowing the value of transcending the consciousness that created the problem.
- Accelerating yourself by multiplying the talents you already have.

- Seeing that that there is something beyond the struggle, something beyond the duality consciousness that has created and that perpetuates the struggle.
- That which is pure is also beautiful.
- A universal sense of beauty, harmony and purity.
- Being willing to accelerate beyond any condition by always seeking to turn the clock forward.
- Willing to question with no sense of taboos or holy cows.
- Cooperation based on the vision of Christ and the underlying oneness of all life.
- Embracing acceleration, flowing with it, adding onto it.
- Adopting a positive outlook on life.
- Seeking to accelerate people's consciousness to the point, where they spontaneously make better choices.
- Letting go of any dualistic standard, and the self defined by such a standard.
- Realizing that the purpose of earth is the growth in self-awareness, not the production of specific outer conditions.
- Realizing that any condition, no matter how impure, can be accelerated into purity.
- No condition is irreversible.
- Knowing that a condition seems real only when viewed from a certain state of consciousness. When you accelerate your consciousness,s you see how unreal a condition is and how easily it can be changed through an acceleration of consciousness.
- Knowing you can be the open door for the fourth ray to accelerate any condition.
- Focusing on raising people's consciousness rather than producing specific material changes.

| *Part Three - Decree vigil*

4.01 DECREE TO ASTREA AND PURITY

In the name I AM THAT I AM, Jesus Christ, I call to my I Will Be Presence to flow through my being and give these decrees with full power. I call to beloved Mighty Astrea and Purity to cut me free from all imperfect energies and all ties to any dark forces or conditions not of the Light, including…

[Make personal calls]

1. Beloved Astrea, your heart is so true,
your Circle and Sword of white and blue,
cut all life free from dramas unwise,
on wings of Purity our planet will rise.

Beloved Astrea, in God Purity,
accelerate all of my life energy,
raising my mind into true unity
with the Masters of love in Infinity.

2. Beloved Astrea, from Purity's Ray,
send forth deliverance to all life today,
acceleration to Purity, I AM now free
from all that is less than love's Purity.

Beloved Astrea, in oneness with you,
your circle and sword of electric blue,
with Purity's Light cutting right through,
raising within me all that is true.

3. Beloved Astrea, accelerate us all,
as for your deliverance I fervently call,
set all life free from vision impure
beyond fear and doubt, I AM rising for sure.

Beloved Astrea, I AM willing to see,
all of the lies that keep me unfree,
I AM rising beyond every impurity,
with Purity's Light forever in me.

4. Beloved Astrea, accelerate life
beyond all duality's struggle and strife,
consume all division between God and man,
accelerate fulfillment of God's perfect plan.

Beloved Astrea, I lovingly call,
break down separation's invisible wall,
I surrender all lies causing the fall,
forever affirming the oneness of All.

Coda:

Accelerate into Purity, I AM real,
Accelerate into Purity, all life heal,
Accelerate into Purity, I AM MORE,
Accelerate into Purity, all will soar.

Accelerate into Purity! (3X)
Beloved Elohim Astrea.

Accelerate into Purity! (3X)
Beloved Gabriel and Hope.

Accelerate into Purity! (3X)
Beloved Serapis Bey.

Accelerate into Purity! (3X)
Beloved I AM.

Sealing:

In the name of the Divine Mother, I fully accept that the power of these calls is used to set free the Ma-ter light, so it can outpicture the perfect vision of Christ for my own life, for all people and for the planet. In the name I AM THAT I AM, it is done! Amen.

4.02 Decree to Archangel Gabriel

In the name I AM THAT I AM, Jesus Christ, I call to my I AM Presence to flow through the I Will Be Presence that I AM and give these decrees with full power. I call to beloved Archangel Gabriel and Hope to shield me in your wings of intense white light, and shatter and cut me free from all imperfect energies and dark forces, including… …

[Make personal calls]

1. Gabriel Archangel, your light I revere,
immersed in your Presence, nothing I fear.
A disciple of Christ, I do leave behind,
the ego's desire for responding in kind.

**Gabriel Archangel, of this I am sure,
Gabriel Archangel, Christ light is the cure.
Gabriel Archangel, intentions so pure,
Gabriel Archangel, in you I'm secure.**

2. Gabriel Archangel, I fear not the light,
in purifications' fire, I delight.
With your hand in mine, each challenge I face,
I follow the spiral to infinite grace.

**Gabriel Archangel, of this I am sure,
Gabriel Archangel, Christ light is the cure.
Gabriel Archangel, intentions so pure,
Gabriel Archangel, in you I'm secure.**

3. Gabriel Archangel, your fire burning white,
ascending with you, out of the night.
My ego has nowhere to run and to hide,
in ascension's bright spiral, with you I abide.

Gabriel Archangel, of this I am sure,
Gabriel Archangel, Christ light is the cure.
Gabriel Archangel, intentions so pure,
Gabriel Archangel, in you I'm secure.

4. Gabriel Archangel, your trumpet I hear,
announcing the birth of Christ drawing near.
In lightness of being, I now am reborn,
rising with Christ on bright Easter morn.

Gabriel Archangel, of this I am sure,
Gabriel Archangel, Christ light is the cure.
Gabriel Archangel, intentions so pure,
Gabriel Archangel, in you I'm secure.

Coda:

With angels I soar,
as I reach for MORE.
The angels so real,
their love all will heal.
The angels bring peace,
all conflicts will cease.
With angels of light,
we soar to new height.

The rustling sound of angel wings,
what joy as even matter sings,
what joy as every atom rings,
in harmony with angel wings.

Sealing:

In the name of the Divine Mother, I fully accept that the power of these calls is used to set free the Ma-ter light, so it can outpicture the perfect vision of Christ for my own life, for all people and for the planet. In the name I AM THAT I AM, it is done! Amen.

PERVERSIONS OF THE FOURTH RAY

- Ultimate impurity is the dualistic standard, which defines opposites and thus obscures the pure reality of God that exists at an entirely higher level.
- Thinking that as long as you do this or don't do that, you must be pure.
- Holding on to an unbalanced expression of one of the first three rays.
- Holding on to the illusion of separateness, seeking to raise the self in comparison to others, even by seeking to put others down.
- Evaluating everything based on the standard of anti-christ instead of the reality of Christ.
- Hypocrisy of thinking one is more pure than others while failing to see it is only according to one's self-centered standard.
- Holding on to comparisons and value judgments, even insisting they represent an absolute truth or God's judgment.
- Saying those who are defined as impure are unworthy or have less value.
- Setting up relative opposites, saying one is better than the other.
- Ignoring the underlying consciousness behind all physical manifestations.
- Defining that other people represent some ultimate threat and thus must be controlled through force or even killed.
- Insisting that one's self-centered perspective has some ultimate status.
- Seeking for an ultimate system that will solve all problems.
- Attempting to solve a problem with the same state of consciousness that created the problem, thinking this can lead to an ultimate solution.
- Waiting for some savior from outside yourself to do the work for you.

- Using your standard, your mental image, to define the problem and then seeking to solve the problem based on that definition rather than accelerating your consciousness to a higher level.
- Appointing a scapegoat as the cause of the problem.
- Holding on to what exists based on a mental image that this is what is supposed to be.
- Seeking to turn the clock back.
- Being unwilling to question existing thought systems and labeling them as infallible or beyond questioning.
- Having intellectual holy cows.
- Refusal to cooperate and instead seeking to force others into compliance with one's present vision.
- Resisting acceleration.
- Holding on to a negative outlook on life.
- Holding on to a dualistic standard, and the self defined by that standard.
- The idea that some ultimate disaster is looming and must be avoided by all means available, even force.

4.03 Decree to Serapis Bey

In the name I AM THAT I AM, Jesus Christ, I call to my I AM Presence to flow through the I Will Be Presence that I AM and give these decrees with full power. I call to beloved Serapis Bey, the other Chohans and the Maha Chohan to release flood tides of light, to consume all blocks and attachments that prevent me from becoming one with the eternal flow of the fourth ray of creative purity and ever-transcending intention, including…

[Make personal calls]

1. Serapis Bey, what power lies,
behind your purifying eyes.
Serapis Bey, it is a treat,
to enter your sublime retreat.

**O Holy Spirit, flow through me,
I am the open door for thee.
O mighty rushing stream of Light,
transcendence is my sacred right.**

2. Serapis Bey, what wisdom found,
your words are always most profound.
Serapis Bey, I tell you true,
my mind has room for naught but you.

**O Holy Spirit, flow through me,
I am the open door for thee.
O mighty rushing stream of Light,
transcendence is my sacred right.**

3. Serapis Bey, what love beyond,
my heart does leap, as I respond.
Serapis Bey, your life a poem,
that calls me to my starry home.

**O Holy Spirit, flow through me,
I am the open door for thee.
O mighty rushing stream of Light,
transcendence is my sacred right.**

4. Serapis Bey, your guidance sure,
my base is clear and white and pure.
Serapis Bey, no longer trapped,
by soul in which my self was wrapped.

**O Holy Spirit, flow through me,
I am the open door for thee.
O mighty rushing stream of Light,
transcendence is my sacred right.**

5. Serapis Bey, what healing balm,
in mind that is forever calm.
Serapis Bey, my thoughts are pure,
your discipline I shall endure.

**O Holy Spirit, flow through me,
I am the open door for thee.
O mighty rushing stream of Light,
transcendence is my sacred right.**

6. Serapis Bey, what secret test,
for egos who want to be best.
Serapis Bey, expose in me,
all that is less than harmony.

**O Holy Spirit, flow through me,
I am the open door for thee.
O mighty rushing stream of Light,
transcendence is my sacred right.**

7. Serapis Bey, what moving sight,
my self ascends to sacred height.
Serapis Bey, forever free,
in sacred synchronicity.

**O Holy Spirit, flow through me,
I am the open door for thee.
O mighty rushing stream of Light,
transcendence is my sacred right.**

8. Serapis Bey, you balance all,
the seven rays upon my call.
Serapis Bey, in space and time,
the pyramid of self, I climb.

**O Holy Spirit, flow through me,
I am the open door for thee.
O mighty rushing stream of Light,
transcendence is my sacred right.**

| *Part Three - Decree vigil*

Sealing:

In the name of the Divine Mother, I fully accept that the power of these calls is used to set free the Ma-ter light, so it can outpicture the perfect vision of Christ for my own life, for all people and for the planet. In the name I AM THAT I AM, it is done! Amen.

The Fifth Ray

Color: **Emerald Green**
Corresponding chakra: **Third eye**

Elohim and their retreat:
Cyclopea and Virginia
Altai Range where China, Siberia and Mongolia meet, near Tabun Bogdo

Archangel, Archeia and their retreat:
Raphael and Mother Mary
Fatima, Portugal

Chohan and his retreat:
Hilarion
Crete, Greece

| *Part Three - Decree vigil*

PURE QUALITIES OF THE FIFTH RAY

- Love for a higher vision, a purer vision, an immaculate vision.
- Seeing beyond current conditions and seeing the potential to transcend those conditions, and manifest a higher vision.
- Seeing that all diverse forms sprang from the same source and substance.
- Seeing that any form is created by projecting a mental image upon the Ma-ter light, which means any form can be transformed.
- Knowing you can never lose your potential to transcend your current form.
- Locking in to the vision of the Elohim and your I AM Presence.
- Willingness to bear witness to the highest truth you can see with your current level of consciousness while seeking to raise your consciousness.
- Willingness to doubt an "absolute" truth and being confused for a while until you being to see a higher vision.
- Knowing that the Spirit of Truth can be expressed in many different ways.
- Knowing that you cannot grasp truth as linear knowledge but only by having a direct experience of the Spirit of Truth, which is beyond believing.
- Knowing that the separate self can never grasp truth but only a relative truth with a dualistic opposite.
- Striving to go beyond duality in order to encounter the indivisible Spirit of Truth.
- Knowing you will always have a localized perspective through the body and outer mind and being and that it can never give you a full view of life.
- Being willing to reach for the perspective of the Christ mind.
- Seeing the difference between an individual, localized perspective and the dualistic, value-laden perspective of the ego.

- Surrendering the ego's desire to have your localized view elevated to some superior or universal status.
- Adopting a neutral approach to life and the spiritual path, so you are always open to the teacher and the Christ mind.
- Realizing the fallacy of trying to prove the superiority of any particular thought system on earth.
- Seeing that truth is the River of Life that is constantly transcending itself.
- Seeing that when you take a quantum leap to a higher level of consciousness, your perception of truth will change.
- Knowing that the absolute truth is the consciousness of the Creator, which is beyond form.
- You can know absolute truth only by coming into oneness with your Creator.
- Realizing that truth cannot be known as an intellectual exercise, but only through gnosis, meaning coming into oneness with the consciousness behind any given form.
- Overcoming the subject-object duality by knowing that it is an illusion created by the ego and the fallen consciousness.
- Seeing that every form created through a matrix in consciousness, and this is what you can come into oneness with through gnosis, whereby you know the form.
- Only through gnosis can you know an objective truth.
- Becoming a clear pane of glass so that the Spirit of Truth can stream through your being.
- Seeing that true healing is wholeness, which comes from gnosis, the oneness with a consciousness greater than your own.
- The willingness to look at your state of consciousness and take full responsibility for it.
- Accepting that regardless of what you encounter in this world, you have the potential to be in command of your own reactions.
- Seeing that the separate self is unreal, and thus the Conscious You can overcome the division between self and other, between self and God.

- Knowing that the separate self seems real only when the Conscious You looks at life from inside the separate self, and that the Conscious You can at any time withdraw itself from this identification.
- Being willing to stop proving that the perception of the separate self is right, and then acknowledging that the separate self is unreal.
- Seeing that the arguments used by the separate self are unreal because they are based on selective perception.
- Giving up the desire to win the argument with the consciousness of anti-christ and simply letting go of the entire struggle.
- Seeking oneness with the Spirit of Truth rather than superiority over the spirit of anti-truth.
- Refusing to let your attention be consumed by the pointless struggle to prove which illusion is more right than any other illusion.
- Seeing that there never will be an ultimate argument and thus simply leaving the struggle behind.
- Being willing to look at the beam in your own eye instead of focusing on the splinter in the eyes of others.
- Seeing that you have had enough of allowing the separate self to consume your attention in a pointless quest for validation.
- Knowing that what you do to others tells the cosmic mirror what you want to experience.
- Seeing the vanity of the dualistic struggle and knowing that you have had enough.
- Being willing to step back from the struggle in order to get the higher vision whereby you can engage in life without struggling.
- Engaging in life with the intention to let your light shine, to share the individuality, the divine individuality, of your I Will Be Presence by always being just the open door and nothing more.
- Seeing the fallacy of acting like a god who can define truth and error, and instead being the open door for the Spirit of Truth to flow through you.

- Being the open door for a perspective based on the oneness of all life.
- Being a co-creator by being the open door for the vision of the Presence.
- Accepting that the Presence has power over matter and thus with God all things are possible.
- Never accepting the reality or permanence of any condition.
- Knowing that any condition is the result of a mental image and can thus be replaced by projecting a higher image.
- Knowing when you have taken on something that is not the highest possible and then striving for a higher vision.
- Seeing the vision of the Elohim and the beauty of life's true potential.
- Focusing on what is possible.
- Letting yourself flow with the realistic optimism of positive people and the ascended masters.
- Affirming your right to live according to a higher vision and express your divine individuality in this world.
- Affirming your right to express your creativity regardless of the opinions of others or current material conditions.
- Never seeking to change others, but giving them a frame of reference that there is a higher choice than the choice they are making right now.

| *Part Three - Decree vigil*

5.01 Decree to Cyclopea and Virginia

In the name I AM THAT I AM, Jesus Christ, I call to my I Will Be Presence to flow through my being and give these decrees with full power. I call to beloved Mighty Cyclopea and Virginia to pierce the illusions of separation and duality, that keep me from attaining wholeness, including…

[Make personal calls]

1. Cyclopea so dear, the truth you reveal,
the truth that duality's ailments will heal,
your Emerald Light is like a great balm,
my emotional body is perfectly calm.

**Cyclopea so dear, in Emerald Sphere,
to vision so clear I always adhere,
in raising perception I shall persevere,
as deep in my heart your truth I revere.**

2. Cyclopea so dear, with you I unwind,
all negative spirals clouding my mind,
I know pure awareness is truly my core,
the key to becoming the wide-open door.

**Cyclopea so dear, clear my inner sight,
empowered, I pierce the soul's fearful night,
through veils of duality I now take flight,
bathed in your penetrating Emerald Light.**

3. Cyclopea so dear, life can only reflect,
the images that my mind does project,
the key to my healing is clearing the mind,
from the images my ego is hiding behind.

**Cyclopea so dear, I want to aim high,
to your healing flame I ever draw nigh,
I now see my life through your single eye,
beyond all disease I AM ready to fly.**

4. Cyclopea so dear, your Emerald Flame,
exposes every subtle, dualistic power game,
including the game of wanting to say,
that truth is defined in only one way.

**Cyclopea so dear, I am feeling the flow,
as your Living Truth upon me you bestow,
I know truth transcends all systems below,
immersed in your light, I continue to grow.**

Coda:

Accelerate into Wholeness, I AM real,
Accelerate into Wholeness, all life heal,
Accelerate into Wholeness, I AM MORE,
Accelerate into Wholeness, all will soar.

Accelerate into Wholeness! (3X)
Beloved Cyclopea and Virginia.

Accelerate into Wholeness! (3X)
Beloved Raphael and Mary.

Accelerate into Wholeness! (3X)
Beloved Master Hilarion.

Accelerate into Wholeness! (3X)
Beloved I AM.

Sealing:

In the name of the Divine Mother, I fully accept that the power of these calls is used to set free the Ma-ter light, so it can outpicture the perfect vision of Christ for my own life, for all people and for the planet. In the name I AM THAT I AM, it is done! Amen.

5.02 Decree to Archangel Raphael

In the name I AM THAT I AM, Jesus Christ, I call to my I AM Presence to flow through the I Will Be Presence that I AM and give these decrees with full power. I call to beloved Archangel Raphael and Mother Mary to shield me in your wings of emerald green light, and shatter and consume all imperfect energies and dark forces, including…

[Make personal calls]

1. Raphael Archangel, your light so intense,
raise me beyond all human pretense.
Mother Mary and you have a vision so bold,
to see that our highest potential unfold.

**Raphael Archangel, for vision I pray,
Raphael Archangel, show me the way,
Raphael Archangel, your emerald ray,
Raphael Archangel, my life a new day.**

2. Raphael Archangel, in emerald sphere,
to immaculate vision I always adhere.
Mother Mary enfolds me in her sacred heart,
from Mother's true love, I am never apart.

**Raphael Archangel, for vision I pray,
Raphael Archangel, show me the way,
Raphael Archangel, your emerald ray,
Raphael Archangel, my life a new day.**

3. Raphael Archangel, all ailments you heal,
each cell in my body in light now you seal.
Mother Mary's immaculate concept I see,
perfection of health is real now for me.

**Raphael Archangel, for vision I pray,
Raphael Archangel, show me the way,
Raphael Archangel, your emerald ray,
Raphael Archangel, my life a new day.**

4. Raphael Archangel, your light is so real,
the vision of Christ in me you reveal.
Mother Mary now helps me to truly transcend,
in emerald light with you I ascend.

**Raphael Archangel, for vision I pray,
Raphael Archangel, show me the way,
Raphael Archangel, your emerald ray,
Raphael Archangel, my life a new day.**

Coda:

With angels I soar,
as I reach for MORE.
The angels so real,
their love all will heal.
The angels bring peace,
all conflicts will cease.
With angels of light,
we soar to new height.

**The rustling sound of angel wings,
what joy as even matter sings,
what joy as every atom rings,
in harmony with angel wings.**

Sealing:

In the name of the Divine Mother, I fully accept that the power of these calls is used to set free the Ma-ter light, so it can outpicture the perfect vision of Christ for my own life, for all people and for the planet. In the name I AM THAT I AM, it is done! Amen.

Perversions of the Fifth Ray

- Thinking that separate forms are separate and separated from their source or thinking some forms are permanent or beyond our power to change.
- Thinking you are bound by an imperfect form and cannot transcend it and denying that there is any vision beyond what you can see with your current level of consciousness.
- Focusing on the worst-case or doomsday scenario, even affirming it as ultimate reality.
- Unwillingness to speak out unless you are sure you have an absolute truth and clinging to what you insist must be the ultimate truth.
- Thinking there must be only one truth and thus only one absolute belief system and agnosticism, thinking it is impossible to know what is true or that there is no higher truth.
- Holding on to the self created from separation and thinking that what this self perceives is reality and failing to see that you have a localized perspective or even thinking it is the same as reality.
- Being blinded by the ego's desire to have your subjective perspective to be a universal perspective and to be accepted as such by other people or even by God.
- Closing your mind to anything that challenges your perception of life, looking only at what validates your view and being attached to a particular thought system and wanting it validated at all cost.
- Wanting to freeze truth in time so it can never change and insisting that truth can be known through the consciousness of separation, by a subject "knowing" the characteristics of a separate object.
- Insisting that the subject-object duality is real and unavoidable.
- Insisting that truth can be defined by a mental image in your mind and denying the possibility of a direct experience of the Spirit of Truth.

- Insisting that because the self is separate from other, it is not responsible for its state of consciousness, because it is a reaction to something forced upon it by the "other."
- Defining truth in such a way that the underlying paradigm is that the self could never be wrong and insisting that the separate self is real.
- Seeking to prove the perception of the separate self right as a camouflage for never seeing the unreality of that self.
- An endless struggle with the perception of the separate selves of other people or the fallen beings and insisting that the separate self is fighting for a greater or worthy cause.
- The desire to prove other people wrong and the fear of being proven wrong or the sense of triumph of being proven right.
- The desire to win some ultimate victory and prove yourself superior and refusing to consider the consequences of the actions of the separate self.
- Believing the illusion the current conditions on earth are real and cannot be changed by you, by the powers of your mind or by the power of the Presence through you.
- Denying your potential to be an open door for the Spirit.
- Focusing on what seems impossible and letting yourself be overpowered by the negativity of other people or dark forces.

5.03 Decree to Hilarion

In the name I AM THAT I AM, Jesus Christ, I call to my I AM Presence to flow through the I Will Be Presence that I AM and give these decrees with full power. I call to beloved Hilarion, the other Chohans and the Maha Chohan to release flood tides of light, to consume all blocks and attachments that prevent me from becoming one with the eternal flow of the fifth ray of creative healing and ever-transcending wholeness, including…

[Make personal calls]

1. Hilarion, on emerald shore,
I'm free from all that's gone before.
Hilarion, I let all go,
that keeps me out of sacred flow.

**O Holy Spirit, flow through me,
I am the open door for thee.
O mighty rushing stream of Light,
transcendence is my sacred right.**

2. Hilarion, the secret key,
is wisdom's own reality.
Hilarion, all life is healed,
the ego's face no more concealed.

**O Holy Spirit, flow through me,
I am the open door for thee.
O mighty rushing stream of Light,
transcendence is my sacred right.**

3. Hilarion, your love for life,
helps me surrender inner strife.
Hilarion, your loving words,
thrill my heart like song of birds.

**O Holy Spirit, flow through me,
I am the open door for thee.
O mighty rushing stream of Light,
transcendence is my sacred right.**

4. Hilarion, invoke the light,
your sacred formulas recite.
Hilarion, your secret tone,
philosopher's most sacred stone.

**O Holy Spirit, flow through me,
I am the open door for thee.
O mighty rushing stream of Light,
transcendence is my sacred right.**

5. Hilarion, with love you greet,
me in your temple over Crete.
Hilarion, your emerald light,
my third eye sees with Christic sight.

**O Holy Spirit, flow through me,
I am the open door for thee.
O mighty rushing stream of Light,
transcendence is my sacred right.**

6. Hilarion, you give me fruit,
of truth that is so absolute.
Hilarion, all stress decrease,
as my ambitions I release.

**O Holy Spirit, flow through me,
I am the open door for thee.
O mighty rushing stream of Light,
transcendence is my sacred right.**

7. Hilarion, my chakras clear,
as I let go of subtlest fear.
Hilarion, I am sincere,
as freedom's truth I do revere.

**O Holy Spirit, flow through me,
I am the open door for thee.
O mighty rushing stream of Light,
transcendence is my sacred right.**

8. Hilarion, you balance all,
the seven rays upon my call.
Hilarion, you keep me true,
as I remain all one with you.

**O Holy Spirit, flow through me,
I am the open door for thee.
O mighty rushing stream of Light,
transcendence is my sacred right.**

Sealing:

In the name of the Divine Mother, I fully accept that the power of these calls is used to set free the Ma-ter light, so it can outpicture the perfect vision of Christ for my own life, for all people and for the planet. In the name I AM THAT I AM, it is done! Amen.

The Sixth Ray

Color: **Purple and gold**
Corresponding chakra: **Solar plexus**

Elohim and their retreat:
Peace and Aloha
Hawaiian islands

Archangel, Archeia and their retreat:
Uriel and Aurora
Tatra Mountains south of Cracow, Poland

Chohan and her retreat:
Lady master Nada
Saudi Arabia

Pure qualities of the Sixth Ray

- Seeing that you do not give service by fighting against anything, for you cannot destroy evil, you can only transcend it.
- Seeing that polarities cannot exist without each other, so relative good can never destroy relative evil.
- Seeing the true polarities of God and expressing them in a balanced manifestation.
- Seeing that true service is to raise your consciousness beyond duality and then help others do the same.
- Seeing the unity beyond the dualistic polarities.
- Seeing that the greatest service is to help humankind begin to see the dualistic struggle and see the difference between the subjective dualistic state of consciousness and the objective universal state of consciousness that is the Christ mind.
- Bringing the Christ perspective into every activity and area of society.
- Seeing that relative good and evil are states of consciousness and thus no people are evil.
- Seeing that all have the potential to step out of the dualistic polarities, and that helping people do this is true service.
- Engaging in the ultimate cause of raising all life.
- Seeing the potential to make a leap beyond duality.
- Seeking to raise consciousness whereby it becomes self-evident that a certain manifestation is unreal, and thus people spontaneously leave it behind.
- Seeing that true peace is a stream of consciousness, a vibration that is completely beyond duality.
- Knowing that peace can only be brought by transcending the dualistic struggle.
- True service is helping people see the illusions of the dualistic struggle.
- Knowing that the only way to bring peace is to walk away from the struggle.

- Engaging in society from the non-attachment of the Middle Way.
- Transcending all desire to use force, instead seeking to awaken people to higher choices.
- Knowing that free will is not the problem.
- Giving people the Christ perspective and then setting them free to make their own choices.
- Knowing that salvation is a matter of raising consciousness, which can only happen voluntarily.
- Seeing that your highest service is to be the open door.
- Seeing that peace is beyond any conditions.
- Seeing beyond surface appearances to the deeper unity between people.
- Seeing beyond a personal agenda and reaching for a greater reality.
- Being an open door for the active stream of peace.
- Standing up for higher unity without going into duality and thus challenging non-peace without polarizing people into opposing factions.
- Knowing the Omega side of peace is soft and soothing.
- Knowing the Alpha side of peace is strong, active and flowing.
- Being willing to stir up things in order to make duality visible, to flush out the serpents.
- Exposing hypocrisy.
- Calming the emotions of self and others.
- Being an open door for the vibration of absolute determination, that will not leave alone those who are trapped in illusion.
- Being willing to bring out other people's anger, even if one becomes the target for that anger.
- Being a mirror that reflects back to people what they are not willing to see in themselves.
- Being an open door for provoking those who are the ultimate hypocrites of thinking they are working for a good cause, while they are truly working to promote the dualistic struggle.

- Being willing to let the flame of peace flush out hidden emotions in yourself, so that you can see them and gradually overcome them.
- Being free from emotions of a lower sort, because you have no agenda, no expectations, you have no cause for which you think you have to fight.
- Being willing to speak out openly and honestly, in a way that is not dualistic.
- Speaking in a way that is neutral, yet active; not passive.
- Speaking in a way that stirs things up in those, who are not willing to look at the beam in their own eye, but always want to focus the debate on the splinters in the eyes of others.
- Being willing to endure even promote a temporary chaos in order to expose the consciousness of anti-peace and give people a choice to leave it behind.
- Being willing to see and transcend divisions in yourself and then using this to help other people do the same.
- Being willing to see if you are not working for a truly good cause but only for a dualistic cause that can never bring true peace.
- Being willing to look at your behavior and ask: "Why are we doing this? Why are we continuing to do this? Have we not had enough of this? Is there not an alternative to this? Is there not a better way?"
- Serving as a personal extension of the cosmic mirror, going into situations and relationships for the purpose of mirroring back to people what is unresolved in their own state of consciousness.
- Allowing people to project upon you, allowing them to abuse you in various ways, as Jesus said: "Resist not evil, but turn the other cheek."
- Being an instrument for people's judgment.
- Being willing to challenge people and their illusions and hypocrisy.
- Knowing that the road to peace might go through chaos and being willing not to leave people in their illusions.

- Being willing to get into peoples faces, so they cannot ignore you or the Christ perspective you bring.
- Being an instrument for getting people to act out what is in their subconscious minds.
- Transcending the warring in your members.
- Standing on the rock of Christ, being unmoved when other attack you.
- Not allowing others to project upon you their unresolved psychology or fallen mindset.
- Being an instrument for challenging the power elite without being destroyed by them or becoming involved with the dualistic struggle.
- Having the courage to embrace the opportunity to serve.
- Seeing that "other people" are not the problem. It is the illusion that there are "other people" that is the problem.

| *Part Three - Decree vigil*

6.01 Decree to Peace and Aloha

In the name I AM THAT I AM, Jesus Christ, I call to my I Will Be Presence to flow through my being and give these decrees with full power. I call to beloved Peace and Aloha to consume all illusions of anti-unity, that keep me tied to conditions and forces that are not one with your Flame of Peace, including…

[Make personal calls]

1. O Elohim Peace, in Unity's Flame,
there is no more room for duality's game,
we know that all form is from the same source,
empowering us to plot a new course.

**O Elohim Peace, the bell now you ring,
causing all atoms to vibrate and sing,
I now see that there is no separate thing,
to my ego-based self I no longer cling.**

2. O Elohim Peace, you help me to know,
that Jesus has come your Flame to bestow,
upon all who are ready to give up the strife,
by following Christ into infinite life.

**O Elohim Peace, through your eyes I see,
that only in oneness will I ever be free,
I give up the sense of a separate me,
I AM crossing Samsara's turbulent sea.**

3. O Elohim Peace, you show me the way,
for clearing my mind from duality's fray,
you pierce the illusions of both time and space,
separation consumed by your Infinite Grace.

O Elohim Peace, what beauty your name,
consuming within me duality's shame,
It was through the vibration of your Golden Flame,
that Christ the illusion of death overcame.

4. O Elohim Peace, you bring now to Earth,
the unstoppable flame of Cosmic Rebirth,
I give up the sense that something is mine,
allowing your Light through my being to shine.

O Elohim Peace, through your tranquility,
we are free from the chaos of duality,
in oneness with God a new identity,
we are raising the Earth into Infinity.

Coda:

Accelerate into Unity, I AM real,
Accelerate into Unity, all life heal,
Accelerate into Unity, I AM MORE,
Accelerate into Unity, all will soar.

Accelerate into Unity! (3X)
Beloved Peace and Aloha.

Accelerate into Unity! (3X)
Beloved Uriel and Aurora.

Accelerate into Unity! (3X)
Beloved Jesus and Nada.

Accelerate into Unity! (3X)
Beloved I AM.

Sealing:

In the name of the Divine Mother, I fully accept that the power of these calls is used to set free the Ma-ter light, so it can outpicture the perfect vision of Christ for my own life, for all people and for the planet. In the name I AM THAT I AM, it is done! Amen.

| *Part Three - Decree vigil*

6.02 Decree to Archangel Uriel

In the name I AM THAT I AM, Jesus Christ, I call to my I AM Presence to flow through the I Will Be Presence that I AM and give these decrees with full power. I call to beloved Archangel Uriel and Aurora to shield me in your wings of purple and golden light, and shatter and consume all imperfect energies and dark forces, including…

[Make personal calls]

> 1. Uriel Archangel, immense is the power,
> of angels of peace, all war to devour.
> The demons of war, no match for your light,
> consuming them all, with radiance so bright.

> **Uriel Archangel, use your great sword,**
> **Uriel Archangel, consume all discord,**
> **Uriel Archangel, we're of one accord,**
> **Uriel Archangel, we walk with the Lord.**

> 2. Uriel Archangel, intense is the sound,
> when millions of angels, their voices compound.
> They build a crescendo, piercing the night,
> life's glorious oneness revealed to our sight.

> **Uriel Archangel, use your great sword,**
> **Uriel Archangel, consume all discord,**
> **Uriel Archangel, we're of one accord,**
> **Uriel Archangel, we walk with the Lord.**

> 3. Uriel Archangel, from out the Great Throne,
> your millions of trumpets, sound the One Tone.
> Consuming all discord with your harmony,
> the sound of all sounds will set all life free.

Uriel Archangel, use your great sword,
Uriel Archangel, consume all discord,
Uriel Archangel, we're of one accord,
Uriel Archangel, we walk with the Lord.

4. Uriel Archangel, all war is now gone,
for you bring a message, from heart of the One.
The hearts of all men, now singing in peace,
the spirals of love, forever increase.

Uriel Archangel, use your great sword,
Uriel Archangel, consume all discord,
Uriel Archangel, we're of one accord,
Uriel Archangel, we walk with the Lord.

Coda:

With angels I soar,
as I reach for MORE.
The angels so real,
their love all will heal.
The angels bring peace,
all conflicts will cease.
With angels of light,
we soar to new height.

The rustling sound of angel wings,
what joy as even matter sings,
what joy as every atom rings,
in harmony with angel wings.

Sealing:

In the name of the Divine Mother, I fully accept that the power of these calls is used to set free the Ma-ter light, so it can outpicture the perfect vision of Christ for my own life, for all people and for the planet. In the name I AM THAT I AM, it is done! Amen.

Perversions of the Sixth Ray

- Letting your good intentions deceive you into working for a false cause that works against peace and thinking the ultimate service is to fight and win the epic struggle against what you define as evil.
- Letting your life be consumed by the impossible quest to annihilate evil and insisting that serving an ultimate cause necessitates fighting against other people or belief systems.
- Being blinded by the division between good and evil and dividing people into those who are good and those who are evil or thinking you have to fight for peace by killing other people.
- The illusion of a war to end all wars or thinking that if we just keep struggling, we will one day have peace.
- Thinking that war can bring peace, that it is possible to have a final war or a final battle, that would bring true and permanent peace to earth.
- Attachment to fighting a good cause and thinking that service must be given through force, seeking to force people to be saved.
- Thinking free will is the problem and thus it is necessary and justifiable to force people to make certain choices.
- Thinking peace can be brought only by forcing people to conform to your conditions and polarizing a debate around extreme positions that make it impossible to come to a consensus.
- Pursuing a subjective agenda instead of looking for a higher vision that unites.
- Endless discussions that lead nowhere but only feed energy to dark forces.
- Unwillingness to look for deeper principles that unite people.
- Focus on surface appearances that divide people into factions.
- Thinking peace is passive, soft, gentle, non-disturbing.
- Submitting to authority or demanding that other people submit in the name of peace.

- Being good according to a dualistic definition.
- The hypocrisy of claiming to be good while in reality pursuing a selfish agenda.
- Accusing others of what oneself is doing.
- Thinking inharmonious emotions are justified.
- Directing *your* anger at other people and saying they are responsible for creating the anger in you and thus deserve to receive what they get.
- Thinking that in order to be spiritual, you have to be calm, gentle, soothing, you have to always be in control—or at least appear to be in control.
- The illusion that winning a final, epic battle will bring peace.
- The illusion that violence and force can bring peace, and thus violence is justified in this particular case.
- The threat of some looming disaster that justifies actions we know would otherwise be wrong.
- The grand illusion that there is an inherent flaw in God's design for the universe. Something has gone wrong, and it needs to be corrected—and we are the ones who must do so according to our perception.

6.03 Decree to Lady Master Nada

In the name I AM THAT I AM, Jesus Christ, I call to my I AM Presence to flow through the I Will Be Presence that I AM and give these decrees with full power. I call to beloved Master Nada, the other Chohans and the Maha Chohan to release flood tides of light, to consume all blocks and attachments that prevent me from becoming one with the eternal flow of the sixth ray of creative peace and ever-transcending service, including…

[Make personal calls]

1. Master Nada, beauty's power,
unfolding like a sacred flower.
Master Nada, so sublime,
a will that conquers even time.

**O Holy Spirit, flow through me,
I am the open door for thee.
O mighty rushing stream of Light,
transcendence is my sacred right.**

2. Master Nada, you bestow,
upon me wisdom's rushing flow.
Master Nada, mind so strong
rising on your wings of song.

**O Holy Spirit, flow through me,
I am the open door for thee.
O mighty rushing stream of Light,
transcendence is my sacred right.**

3. Master Nada, precious scent,
your love is truly heaven-sent.
Master Nada, kind and soft
on wings of love we rise aloft.

**O Holy Spirit, flow through me,
I am the open door for thee.
O mighty rushing stream of Light,
transcendence is my sacred right.**

4. Master Nada, mother light,
my heart is rising like a kite.
Master Nada, from your view,
all life is pure as morning dew.

**O Holy Spirit, flow through me,
I am the open door for thee.
O mighty rushing stream of Light,
transcendence is my sacred right.**

5. Master Nada, truth you bring,
as morning birds in love do sing.
Master Nada, I now feel,
your love that all four bodies heal.

**O Holy Spirit, flow through me,
I am the open door for thee.
O mighty rushing stream of Light,
transcendence is my sacred right.**

6. Master Nada, serve in peace,
as all emotions I release.
Master Nada, life is fun,
my solar plexus is a sun.

**O Holy Spirit, flow through me,
I am the open door for thee.
O mighty rushing stream of Light,
transcendence is my sacred right.**

7. Master Nada, love is free,
with no conditions binding me.
Master Nada, rise above,
all human forms of lesser love.

**O Holy Spirit, flow through me,
I am the open door for thee.
O mighty rushing stream of Light,
transcendence is my sacred right.**

8. Master Nada, balance all,
the seven rays upon my call.
Master Nada, rise and shine,
your radiant beauty most divine.

**O Holy Spirit, flow through me,
I am the open door for thee.
O mighty rushing stream of Light,
transcendence is my sacred right.**

Sealing:

In the name of the Divine Mother, I fully accept that the power of these calls is used to set free the Ma-ter light, so it can outpicture the perfect vision of Christ for my own life, for all people and for the planet. In the name I AM THAT I AM, it is done! Amen.

MORE PERVERSIONS OF THE SIXTH RAY

- Unwillingness to confront divisions, seeking to gloss them over and create the appearance of peace.
- Helping to camouflage and perpetuate the dualistic struggle by not seeing the illusions of anti-peace.
- Insisting that we have to continue doing what we have always been doing and that this will eventually bring peace.
- Denying that staying in illusion will lead to self-destruction, insisting there must be a way out.
- Thinking you are so good that you are guaranteed to be saved.
- Denying that what you are doing demonstrates you have unresolved problems in your subconscious mind, instead projecting that what you do is necessary or justified because others are doing something wrong.
- Denying that there is warring in your members.
- Letting other people's behavior or projections take away your inner peace and enjoying the battle with others.
- Always projecting that other people are the problem.

The Seventh Ray

Color: **Violet**

Corresponding chakra: **Seat of the soul or innocence chakra**

Elohim and their retreat:
Arcturus and Victoria
Near Luanda, Angola, Africa

Archangel, Archeia and their retreat:
Zadkiel and Holy Amethyst
Cuba

Chohan and his retreat:
Saint Germain
*Transylvania, Romania and
Table Mountain, Rocky Mountains, U.S.A.*

PURE QUALITIES OF THE SEVENTH RAY

- Seeing freedom as the opportunity to transcend the self one has—in any way that the self one has can imagine and conceive of.
- Seeing that freedom truly is completely unrestricted by God or the ascended masters. Thus only the ego and dark forces seek to restrict your freedom.
- Understanding that neither the Creator nor any representative of the mind of Christ would do anything to limit your knowledge, understanding, vision or imagination.
- Knowing that God has given you a sense of self, and God has given you complete freedom as to what to do with that sense of self here in the material realm.
- Seeing that the basis for freedom is imagination, for you cannot attain what you cannot imagine.
- Knowing that you cannot be truly free, if your imagination is restricted within a certain framework or mental box.
- Knowing that your current mental box cannot be used to imagine what is beyond the box.
- Daring to express your true individuality.
- Seeing that you are ultimately free, when the Conscious You has disentangled itself from the separate self, so that you are no longer perceiving everything through the filter of the separate self.
- Knowing you are free when the Conscious You comes to the recognition: "I am that I am; I am THAT I am up there, and not the separate I am down here."
- Knowing that ultimate freedom is oneness with the I AM Presence, is being the I Will Be aspect of the Presence.
- Acknowledging that you have complete freedom as to where you focus your attention.
- Knowing that your Presence can express its creativity through any activity you choose.

- Transcending the fear-based mindset so you no longer see the fallen beings or dark forces as a threat to you.
- Knowing that the real key to freedom is to take command over your state of mind, so you are not allowing the fallen beings to intimidate you into voluntarily restricting the expression of your individuality, your Christhood.
- Knowing that no force in the material world can stop your self-transcendence.
- Seeing through the serpentine lies, so you do not voluntarily restrict your freedom and creativity.
- Knowing that the Ma-ter light can take on any form, and thus the material world cannot restrict your creative freedom.
- Overcoming the fear of freedom, by recognizing that you have the capacity and the right to define your sense of self any way you want. And that you define the self based on your I AM Presence.
- Knowing that by letting the separate self die, you will not die. There will be something left.
- Overcoming the fear of death, the fear that the separate self could be no more by surrendering into death.
- Overcoming fear by looking at what you fear, going right into the fear and then experiencing how unreal it is.
- Knowing that nothing you fear can change who you are as a spiritual being, and thus there really is no reason to fear it.
- Knowing that the Conscious You is immortal, whereas any condition on earth is only temporary.
- Knowing that when you survive physical death, there is nothing you need to fear.
- Knowing there is nothing you cannot transcend by choosing to let the old self die.
- Knowing that you can attain peace of mind regardless of the temporary conditions you face on earth.

| *Part Three - Decree vigil*

7.01 DECREE TO ELOHIM ARCTURUS AND VICTORIA

In the name I AM THAT I AM, Jesus Christ, I call to my I Will Be Presence to flow through my being and give these decrees with full power. I call to beloved Mighty Arcturus and Victoria to release an infinite flow of Violet Flame to transform all conditions not of the light in my consciousness and world, including…

[Make personal calls]

1. Beloved Arcturus, release now the flow,
of Violet Flame to help all life grow,
in ever-expanding circles of Light,
it pulses within every atom so bright.

**Beloved Arcturus, thou Elohim Free,
I open my heart to your reality,
expanding my heart into Infinity,
your flame is the key to my God-victory.**

2. Beloved Arcturus, be with me alway,
reborn, I am ready to face a new day,
I have no attachments to life here on Earth,
I claim a new life in your Flame of Rebirth.

**Beloved Arcturus, your Violet Flame pure,
is for every ailment the ultimate cure,
against it no darkness could ever endure,
my freedom it will forever ensure.**

3. Beloved Arcturus, your bright violet fire,
now fills every atom, raising them higher,
the space in each atom all filled with your light,
as matter itself is shining so bright.

> Beloved Arcturus, your transforming Grace,
> empowers me now every challenge to face,
> as your violet light floods my inner space,
> towards my ascension I willingly race.

> 4. Beloved Arcturus, bring in a new age,
> help Earth and humanity turn a new page,
> your transforming light gives me certainty,
> Saint Germain's Golden Age is a reality.

> **Beloved Arcturus, I surrender all fear,
> I AM feeling your Presence so tangibly near,
> with your Freedom's Song filling my ear,
> I know that to God I AM ever so dear.**

Coda:

> Accelerate into Freedom, I AM real,
> Accelerate into Freedom, all life heal,
> Accelerate into Freedom, I AM MORE,
> Accelerate into Freedom, all will soar.

> **Accelerate into Freedom! (3X)**
> Beloved Arcturus and Victoria.

> **Accelerate into Freedom! (3X)**
> Beloved Zadkiel and Amethyst.

> **Accelerate into Freedom! (3X)**
> Beloved Saint Germain.

> **Accelerate into Freedom! (3X)**
> Beloved I AM.

Sealing:

In the name of the Divine Mother, I fully accept that the power of these calls is used to set free the Ma-ter light, so it can outpicture the perfect vision of Christ for my own life, for all people and for the planet. In the name I AM THAT I AM, it is done! Amen.

7.02 Decree to Archangel Zadkiel and Holy Amethyst

In the name I AM THAT I AM, Jesus Christ, I call to my I AM Presence to flow through the I Will Be Presence that I AM and give these decrees with full power. I call to beloved Archangel Zadkiel and Holy Amethyst to shield me in your wings of intense violet light, and shatter and transmute all imperfect energies and dark forces, including...

[Make personal calls]

1. Zadkiel Archangel, your flow is so swift,
in your violet light, I instantly shift,
into a vibration in which I am free,
from all limitations of the lesser me.

**Zadkiel Archangel, encircle the earth,
Zadkiel Archangel, with your violet girth,
Zadkiel Archangel, unstoppable mirth,
Zadkiel Archangel, our planet's rebirth.**

2. Zadkiel Archangel, I truly aspire,
to being the master of your violet fire.
Wielding the power, of your alchemy,
I use Sacred Word, to set all life free.

**Zadkiel Archangel, encircle the earth,
Zadkiel Archangel, with your violet girth,
Zadkiel Archangel, unstoppable mirth,
Zadkiel Archangel, our planet's rebirth.**

3. Zadkiel Archangel, your violet light,
transforming the earth, with unstoppable might.
So swiftly our planet, beginning to spin,
with legions of angels, our victory we win.

**Zadkiel Archangel, encircle the earth,
Zadkiel Archangel, with your violet girth,
Zadkiel Archangel, unstoppable mirth,
Zadkiel Archangel, our planet's rebirth.**

4. Zadkiel Archangel, your violet flame,
the earth and humanity, never the same.
Saint Germain's Golden Age, is a reality,
what glorious wonder, I joyously see.

**Zadkiel Archangel, encircle the earth,
Zadkiel Archangel, with your violet girth,
Zadkiel Archangel, unstoppable mirth,
Zadkiel Archangel, our planet's rebirth.**

Coda:

With angels I soar,
as I reach for MORE.
The angels so real,
their love all will heal.
The angels bring peace,
all conflicts will cease.
With angels of light,
we soar to new height.

**The rustling sound of angel wings,
what joy as even matter sings,
what joy as every atom rings,
in harmony with angel wings.**

Sealing:

In the name of the Divine Mother, I fully accept that the power of these calls is used to set free the Ma-ter light, so it can outpicture the perfect vision of Christ for my own life, for all people and for the planet. In the name I AM THAT I AM, it is done! Amen.

| *Part Three - Decree vigil*

PERVERSIONS OF THE SEVENTH RAY

The primary perversion of the seventh ray qualities is a tendency to take life very seriously. This can be expressed as a perversion of both freedom and justice, which combines into the sense that you live in a world where everything is a struggle, perhaps even a struggle against a force that is unjustly seeking to take away your freedom.

The extreme perversion of the seventh ray is the epic mindset, where one thinks the world is locked in an epic battle between good and evil, meaning that anything can be justified in the fight to destroy evil. This leads to complete insensitivity towards life, which has led to some of the worst examples of human cruelty. Yet, as with everything else, insensitivity towards others comes from an insensitivity towards oneself.

When you have perverted the seventh ray qualities, you tend to think that the problems in the world exist because other people don't take them as seriously as you do. As you overcome this imbalance, you realize that the conditions are still here because people take them too seriously, thus thinking the conditions of the material world have power over their Spirits. In reality, we are all spiritual beings, and one of our ultimate tasks on earth is to demonstrate that we will not allow material conditions to limit our Spirits and their expression in this world.

• Defining the self according to conditions or earth, and saying this is the only way the self can be and seeking to limit imagination or labeling specific ideas a dangerous.
• Thinking that in order to be saved or serve some ultimate cause, you should suppress individuality, your creative expression of that individuality, in order to comply with a standard defined by the fallen beings.
• Seeing the freedom and the light of others as a threat—and then seeking to restrict their light through force or deception.

- Thinking your freedom and creative expression is limited by the fallen beings and dark forces and rebelling against all real or perceived limitations of your freedom.
- Thinking your freedom is limited by the material world.
- Running away from or denying the fear that the separate self can die, by clinging to the belief that something on earth will make the separate self worthy to enter heaven.
- Running away from the fear of being able to create anything you want, by insisting that something on earth limits your creative freedom.
- Fighting the death of the separate self by clinging to a false sense of life.
- Spending your entire life on seeking to avoid something.
- Spending your life running away from what you fear, because you are afraid to look at it.
- Fearing that you might have to suffer a certain condition for all eternity—even though you also fear that you could die.
- Fearing that certain choices will cause you to suffer or be trapped forever.
- Fearing that something on earth can take away your peace of mind.

7.03 Decree to Saint Germain

In the name I AM THAT I AM, Jesus Christ, I call to my I AM Presence to flow through the I Will Be Presence that I AM and give these decrees with full power. I call to beloved Saint Germain and Portia, the other Chohans and the Maha Chohan to release flood tides of light, to consume all blocks and attachments that prevent me from becoming one with the eternal flow of the seventh ray of creative freedom and ever-transcending oneness, including…

[Make personal calls]

1. Saint Germain, your alchemy,
with violet fire now sets me free.
Saint Germain, I ever grow,
in freedom's overpowering flow.

**O Holy Spirit, flow through me,
I am the open door for thee.
O mighty rushing stream of Light,
transcendence is my sacred right.**

2. Saint Germain, your mastery,
of violet flame geometry.
Saint Germain, in you I see,
the formulas that set me free.

**O Holy Spirit, flow through me,
I am the open door for thee.
O mighty rushing stream of Light,
transcendence is my sacred right.**

3. Saint Germain, in Liberty,
I feel the love you have for me.
Saint Germain, I do adore,
the violet flame that makes all more.

**O Holy Spirit, flow through me,
I am the open door for thee.
O mighty rushing stream of Light,
transcendence is my sacred right.**

4. Saint Germain, in unity,
I will transcend duality.
Saint Germain, my self so pure,
your violet chemistry so sure.

**O Holy Spirit, flow through me,
I am the open door for thee.
O mighty rushing stream of Light,
transcendence is my sacred right.**

5. Saint Germain, reality,
in violet light I am carefree.
Saint Germain, my aura seal,
your violet flame my chakras heal.

**O Holy Spirit, flow through me,
I am the open door for thee.
O mighty rushing stream of Light,
transcendence is my sacred right.**

6. Saint Germain, your chemistry,
with violet fire set atoms free.
Saint Germain, from lead to gold,
transforming vision I behold.

**O Holy Spirit, flow through me,
I am the open door for thee.
O mighty rushing stream of Light,
transcendence is my sacred right.**

7. Saint Germain, transcendency,
as I am always one with thee.
Saint Germain, from soul I'm free,
I so delight in being me.

**O Holy Spirit, flow through me,
I am the open door for thee.
O mighty rushing stream of Light,
transcendence is my sacred right.**

8. Saint Germain, nobility,
the key to sacred alchemy.
Saint Germain, you balance all,
the seven rays upon my call.

**O Holy Spirit, flow through me,
I am the open door for thee.
O mighty rushing stream of Light,
transcendence is my sacred right.**

| *Part Three - Decree vigil*

Sealing:

In the name of the Divine Mother, I fully accept that the power of these calls is used to set free the Ma-ter light, so it can outpicture the perfect vision of Christ for my own life, for all people and for the planet. In the name I AM THAT I AM, it is done! Amen.

The Eight Ray

Color: between pink and gold; a **peach color**

Corresponding chakra: **Secret chamber of the Heart**

Archangel:

Uzziel

Chohan and his retreat:

Maha Chohan

Sri Lanka, Ceylon

8.01 Decree to Maha Chohan

In the name I AM THAT I AM, Jesus Christ, I call to my I Will Be Presence to flow through my being and give these decrees with full power. I call to beloved Maha Chohan and the seven Chohans to release flood tides of light, to consume all blocks and attachments that prevent me from flowing with the River of Life and transcending myself daily, including…

[Make personal calls]

1. Maha Chohan, I will to grow,
I feel the power of your flow.
Maha Chohan, the veil is rent,
creative will from heaven sent.

**O Holy Spirit, flow through me,
I am the open door for thee.
O mighty rushing stream of Light,
transcendence is my sacred right.**

2. Maha Chohan, your wisdom streams,
awaken all from matter's dreams.
Maha Chohan, your balance bring,
let bells of integration ring.

**O Holy Spirit, flow through me,
I am the open door for thee.
O mighty rushing stream of Light,
transcendence is my sacred right.**

3. Maha Chohan, love's mighty call,
the prison walls are shattered all.
Maha Chohan, set all life free
through unconditionality.

**O Holy Spirit, flow through me,
I am the open door for thee.
O mighty rushing stream of Light,
transcendence is my sacred right.**

4. Maha Chohan, intentions pure,
all life is one, I know for sure.
Maha Chohan, I am awake,
surrender all for oneness' sake.

**O Holy Spirit, flow through me,
I am the open door for thee.
O mighty rushing stream of Light,
transcendence is my sacred right.**

5. Maha Chohan, help all men see,
through veils of unreality.
Maha Chohan, with single eye,
I know I am the greater "I."

**O Holy Spirit, flow through me,
I am the open door for thee.
O mighty rushing stream of Light,
transcendence is my sacred right.**

6. Maha Chohan, your peace I find,
Maitreya shows me to be kind.
Maha Chohan, all war will cease,
now flooding all with sacred peace.

**O Holy Spirit, flow through me,
I am the open door for thee.
O mighty rushing stream of Light,
transcendence is my sacred right.**

7. Maha Chohan, you balance all,
the seven rays upon my call.
Maha Chohan, all life is free,
transcending for eternity.

**O Holy Spirit, flow through me,
I am the open door for thee.
O mighty rushing stream of Light,
transcendence is my sacred right.**

8. Maha Chohan, your sacred Flame,
what beauty in your blessed name.
Maha Chohan, what rushing flow,
the Spirit one with life below.

**O Holy Spirit, flow through me,
I am the open door for thee.
O mighty rushing stream of Light,
transcendence is my sacred right.**

| *Part Three - Decree vigil*

Sealing:

In the name of the Divine Mother, I fully accept that the power of these calls is used to set free the Ma-ter light, so it can outpicture the perfect vision of Christ for my own life, for all people and for the planet. In the name I AM THAT I AM, it is done! Amen.